W9-BLE-158

THE MATHEMATICS
OF INVESTING

THE MATHEMATICS OF INVESTING

A Complete Reference

Michael C. Thomsett

WILEY

John Wiley & Sons

New York Chichester Brisbane Toronto Singapore

Copyright © 1989 by John Wiley & Sons

All rights reserved. Published simultaneously in Canada.

Reproduction or translation of any part of this work
beyond that permitted by Section 107 or 108 of the
1976 United States Copyright Act without the permission
of the copyright owner is unlawful. Requests for
permission or further information should be addressed to
the Permissions Department, John Wiley & Sons, Inc.

This publication is designed to provide accurate and
authoritative information in regard to the subject
matter covered. It is sold with the understanding that
the publisher is not engaged in rendering legal, accounting,
or other professional service. If legal advice or other
expert assistance is required, the services of a competent
professional person should be sought. *From a Declaration
of Principles jointly adopted by a Committee of the
American Bar Association and a Committee of Publishers.*

Library of Congress Cataloging-in-Publication Data:
Thomsett, Michael C.
    The mathematics of investing / Michael C. Thomsett.
      p.   cm.
    Bibliography: p.
    Includes index.
    ISBN 0-471-50664-8
    1. Investments—Mathematics. 2. Business mathematics. I. Title.
HG4515.3.T46   1989
332.6'01'51—dc20   89-16458
                                                                   CIP

Printed in the United States of America

Contents

List of Investment Formulas

THE MATHEMATICS
OF INVESTING

Introduction

Yield is the score that investors keep, and math is the scorekeeper's tool. Only by mastering the concepts of investment math can you accurately judge your own performance.

As an investor, you must contend with many problems and decisions: the selection of products that fit your defined risk level, identification of sources for information and advice, and constant research into the dynamic and diverse markets available to you. At the same time, you must be able to translate information from the language spoken by the investment community—the scorekeeping language of returns, yields, and time value of money—into tangible and specific decisions.

This book identifies the concepts on which investment definitions are founded, and on which judgments are made. The timing of a purchase and, even more critically, of a sale, appears at first a relatively simple idea. You buy investments with potential for growth or income, and sell when that objective has been achieved; or, as it is more commonly expressed, buy low and sell high.

If you have compared two unlike investments in depth, you already know that timing and selection are not simple matters. So much depends on matching understood levels of risk (in its many forms) with a predetermined acceptable level of return. That involves not only yield on your initial investment, but the time required and the amount of money needed as an initial deposit.

We will present the methods used for translating your investment objectives into measurable terms, beginning with a discussion and explanation of the time value of money (Chapter 1). In order to put those ideas to work, you will need to become familiar with the six common interest tables (Chapter 2), and the many forms of expressing rates of return (Chapter 3). Additional factors affecting the real rate of return are taxes and inflation (Chapter 4).

Following these chapters is a discussion of fundamental and technical analysis and the mathematical implications of those techniques (Chapters 5 through 8).

Next is a series of chapters dealing with the math unique to specialized markets: options and futures, bonds, mutual funds, pooled investments, and real estate (Chapters 9 through 12).

The final section of the book discusses retirement math (Chapter 13) and daily applications (Chapter 14). Following this is an appendix summarizing ratios and formulas, and a glossary of terms.

In order to make this book as practical and useful as possible, the following approach has been taken: Each chapter describes broadly the ideas and techniques and, as each is introduced, examples of applications are given. This approach will help you to apply the information to real-life situations. Concepts are difficult to grasp when presented without a context, so great care has been taken to match each idea with the related action.

This approach will help you to apply the scorekeeping techniques of investment math to your own portfolio and personal financial plan; help improve your focus and clarify your investment goals; make valid comparisons between two or more viable choices; and determine the best time to buy as well as to sell.

Complex formulas and abstract ideas have been avoided on the premise that most readers want clear, practical information they can put to use right away. As a result, some formulas described in the following chapters may involve a number of steps that could be expressed with shorter but more complex formulas. However, only a limited number of individuals appreciate these more complex and abbreviated mathematical expressions, and they are more inclined toward academic principles than to practical application. This book is for the individual who needs to apply ideas to situations of immediate urgency. Our intention and motive is to create a series of explanations and examples that will achieve those goals.

1

The Time Value
of Money

Everyone who invests money hopes it will grow to a larger amount in the future. For the speculator, high risks offer the potential for quick and substantial gains—or losses. For the very conservative investor, the near certainty of future value is traded for a lower yield.

Most investors fall somewhere between these extremes. If you are a typical moderate investor, you will not settle for extremely low yields, even when the rate is guaranteed and your principal is insured; and you are equally unwilling to put all of your money into high-risk speculations. So how do you judge an investment? How do you decide which ones represent acceptable risks, and which ones do not? For many, the decision of what to buy is made inconsistently, and the decision of *when* to buy and sell is equally uncertain.

By applying a standard to these decisions, the choice is made clearer and easier. The standard must involve three elements: risk, potential yield, and time.

Risk may involve the potential for loss of capital, uncertainty of interest or dividend rates, future competitive factors, taxes, inflation, liquidity, degree of diversification, and the existence or lack of insurance on an account.

Potential yield depends on the investment product you are reviewing. Some investments offer guaranteed yields, either for a minimum period of time, or until a maturity date. You cannot always refer to historical yield as an indicator of future performance; yet promoters use historical information to sell shares or units.

Time is probably the most overlooked factor in the setting of standards. How long will it take you to realize the growth or income you expect from your investments? A 100 percent return is impressive if earned in a one-year period. But over a 20-year period, it represents only about 3.6 percent per year—less than you can earn in an insured savings account.

Collectively, risk, yield and time can be used to add focus to your investment decisions. Most investors select products based only on historical or potential yield; others make selections based on various forms of risk and potential yield.

Regardless of the method you use to select and time your decisions, one fact remains: There is a widespread emphasis on mathematical expression in investment literature and communication. A review of marketing brochures, prospectuses, financial statements, and research reports reveals this. An informed decision must depend on your ability to comprehend this information and, more critically, to develop a tangible belief based on what the mathematical formula claims.

COMPOUND INTEREST

Investors must deal with a vast array of mathematical claims and promises in investment literature. Many understand the concepts of risk and yield thoroughly; many more overlook the time factor in judging relative risk.

Depositing money in an interest-bearing account is a traditional method for accumulating savings. The benefit accrues over the long term, due to the effects of compound interest. As interest is credited to the account, it then earns interest itself during the following period. Over a long period of time, a modest deposit will grow to a substantial sum. A basic premise of the time value of money is that *the longer the period over which a deposit is left, the greater the benefits of compounding*.

To quickly determine how much time is required to double a sum of money, you can apply an estimate known as the "rule of 72." This is an approximation, since the exact time depends on the compounding method being used.

The rule of 72 is computed in this way: Divide 72 by the stated interest rate, and the answer is the approximate number of years required to double a deposit.

Formula: the Rule of 72

$$\frac{72}{\text{Interest rate}} = \text{Years to double}$$

Example: You deposit $1,000 in an account that pays 6 percent interest. How long will it take, with compound interest, to double to $2,000?

$$\frac{72}{6} = 12$$

It will take approximately 12 years to double your deposit.

While not an exact measurement of time, the rule of 72 is a useful device to quickly judge an interest rate.

Regardless of the interest rate used, the basic formula for its computation must always involve three factors: the principal amount, the rate, and the time involved.

Formula: Interest Calculation

$$I = P \times R \times T,$$

where

I = interest,
P = principal,
R = interest rate,
T = time.

Example: You are comparing three different investments for your portfolio:

1. The first will involve depositing $1,500 for six months at 8 percent interest.
2. The second calls for a $5,000 initial investment for 15 months at 6 percent.
3. The third requires $2,000 for three months and will pay 12 percent.

In order to make a true comparison, the varying time periods must be expressed in terms of an *annual* period. Thus, six months is one-half, or 0.5 of one year; 15 months represents 1.25 years; and three months is equal to one-fourth, or 0.25 of a year:

1. $I = P \times R \times T$
   $= \$1,500 \times 0.08 \times 0.5$
   $= \$60.$

2. $I = P \times R \times T$
   $= \$5,000 \times 0.06 \times 1.25$
   $= \$375.$

3. $I = P \times R \times T$
   $= \$2,000 \times 0.12 \times 0.25$
   $= \$60.$

COMPOUNDING METHODS

Compounding—interest paid on interest—occurs in one of several ways. Daily compounding is a method used by many savings institutions. The annual rate is divided by the days in a year, and the daily rate is then applied to each day's beginning balance.

Daily compounding is computed on either a 365-day or a 360-day basis. The latter assumes that, for the purpose of computing interest, the year consists of 12 months, each with 30 days. The formula for the 365-day method is:

Formula: Daily Compounding

$$\frac{\text{Annual Rate}}{365} = \text{Daily Rate.}$$

Example: Your bank compounds interest on savings accounts on a daily basis, and pays 6.0 percent interest. Each day, your balance is increased by $\frac{1}{365}$ of the stated annual rate:

$$\frac{0.06}{365} = 0.000164.$$

In investment applications other than savings, daily compounding is rarely seen. For this reason, we will concentrate on the more frequently used methods of compounding interest: monthly, quarterly, semiannually, and annually.

Monthly compounding involves dividing the annual interest rate by 12 (months), and then multiplying the principal amount by the proportional rate.

Formula: Monthly Compounding

$$\frac{\text{Annual Rate}}{12} = \text{Monthly Rate.}$$

Example: You deposit $1,000 in an account that pays 6 percent, compounded monthly. The monthly interest rate will be ½ of 1 percent:

$$\frac{6\%}{12} = 0.5\%.$$

Because compounding takes place each month, the true yield per year will be greater than a straight 6 percent. The annual compounded yield for 6 percent is 6.168 percent. A summary of a full year's calculations is shown in Figure 1.1.

Note that each month's interest increases throughout the year. This occurs because interest is being accumulated on an ever-growing balance. Thus, over time, the account's value will grow at an accelerating rate.

The effects of compounding $1,000 at 0.5% per month over a number of years are impressive:

$$
\begin{aligned}
20 \text{ years} &= \$\ 3,310; \\
30 \text{ years} &= \ \ \ 6,023; \\
40 \text{ years} &= \ \ 10,957; \\
50 \text{ years} &= \ \ 19,936.
\end{aligned}
$$

Quarterly compounding involves four periods per year. Interest is accrued at a rate equal to one-fourth of the stated annual rate. For example, at 6 percent interest, a deposit earns 1.5 percent at the end of each quarter. This is illustrated in Figure 1.2.

With quarterly compounding, a $1,000 deposit in a 6 percent account earns only 32 cents less than in an account where interest is compounded monthly; but at the end of longer terms, the compounding method makes a large difference. At 6 percent, $1,000 compounded quarterly will grow to:

MONTH	6% INTEREST	BALANCE
		1,000.00
1	5.00	1,005.00
2	5.02	1,010.02
3	5.05	1,015.07
4	5.08	1,020.15
5	5.10	1,025.25
6	5.13	1,030.38
7	5.15	1,035.53
8	5.18	1,040.71
9	5.20	1,045.91
10	5.23	1,051.14
11	5.26	1,056.40
12	5.28	1,061.68

FIGURE 1.1 Compound interest—monthly.

MONTH	6% INTEREST	BALANCE
		1,000.00
3	15.00	1,015.00
6	15.22	1,030.22
9	15.45	1,045.67
12	15.69	1,061.36

FIGURE 1.2   Compound interest—quarterly.

20 years = $ 3,291;
30 years =   5,969;
40 years =   10,828;
50 years =   19,643.

Compounding may also be figured semiannually. With this method, the annual rate is divided by two, and interest is accrued at one-half the annual rate, paid every six months. This method is shown in Figure 1.3.

The last compounding method is done annually. With this approach, a deposit is credited with the stated rate of interest at the end of each 12-month period, as shown in Figure 1.4.

A comparison of the effects of different compounding methods over a long period of time is shown in the table below.

Compounding Methods

YEAR	Compounding Method			
	MONTHLY	QUARTERLY	SEMIANNUALLY	ANNUALLY
20	$ 3,310	$ 3,291	$ 3,262	$ 3,207
30	6,023	5,969	5,892	5,743
40	10,957	10,828	10,641	10,286
50	19,936	19,643	19,219	18,420

MONTH	6% INTEREST	BALANCE
		1,000.00
6	30.00	1,030.00
12	30.90	1,060.90
18	31.83	1,092.73
24	32.78	1,125.51

FIGURE 1.3   Compound interest—semiannually.

MONTH	6% INTEREST	BALANCE
		1,000.00
12	60.00	1,060.00
24	63.60	1,123.60
36	67.42	1,191.02
48	71.46	1,262.48

FIGURE 1.4   Compound interest—annually.

The Accumulated Value of 1

Calculating compound interest for one year is a fairly easy task, once the method is understood. Annual compounding involves multiplying the amount on deposit by the stated annual rate; and carrying the new balance forward to the following year. Semiannual compounding requires dividing the annual rate by two, and computing interest twice per year. Quarterly compounding involves four annual computations at one-fourth the annual rate. And monthly compounding calls for 12 calculations, one for each month.

This exercise becomes more involved when interest must be calculated over periods greater than one or two years. If you must compute monthly compounding for a deposit over a 20-year period, it will involve 240 steps.

In the following section and for the remainder of this chapter, the formulas for calculating six types of compound interest will be presented and explained. The task is simplified by referring to widely published compound interest tables, which are thoroughly explained in the next chapter. For now, our objective is not to explain how to use tables, but to show the underlying methods for the calculations themselves.

If tables exist, why bother with the details? The reasoning is that the tables and their terminology are confusing unless the idea behind each table is first explained, examined, and proven. The following formulas show how each of the six types of interest are figured.

The first calculation is for the accumulated value of 1, which describes the steps involved in computing compound interest for any length of time. The "1" refers to a single dollar left on deposit. A factor is developed from the formula, and then applied to the full amount to be deposited.

A good way to understand a formula is to begin with a question. The accumulated value of 1 is the answer to the question:

What will a single deposit be worth after n periods, assuming r interest?

The accumulated (or, future) value is expressed as:

Formula: Accumulated Value of 1

$$AV = D (1 + r)^n$$

where
AV = accumulated value,
D = deposit,
r = interest rate,
n = number of periods.

For computing monthly interest at 6 percent, the formula must take into account the division of the annual rate. Thus:

$$AV = 1 \left(1 + \frac{0.06}{12}\right)^{12}$$

When reduced to its simplified form, this expression may be stated as:

$$AV = 1 (1 + 0.005)^{12}.$$

The factor "1" is replaced by the amount of the deposit, and the number of periods can be expressed as a series of factors.

Example: The accumulated value of a $1,000 deposit at 6 percent, for four compounding periods, is expressed as:

Monthly Compounding, 4 Months

$$
\begin{aligned}
AV &= 1,000 (1 + 0.005)^4 \\
&= 1,000 (1.005)(1.005)(1.005)(1.005) \\
&= 1,000 (1.02015) \\
&= 1,020.15.
\end{aligned}
$$

Quarterly Compounding, 4 Quarters

$$
\begin{aligned}
AV &= 1,000 (1 + 0.015)^4 \\
&= 1,000 (1.015)(1.015)(1.015)(1.015) \\
&= 1,000 (1.06136) \\
&= 1,061.36.
\end{aligned}
$$

Semiannual Compounding, 2 Years

$$
\begin{aligned}
AV &= 1,000 (1 + 0.03)^4 \\
&= 1,000 (1.03)(1.03)(1.03)(1.03)
\end{aligned}
$$

$$= 1,000 \ (1.12551)$$
$$= 1,125.51.$$

Annual Compounding, 4 Years

$$AV = 1,000 \ (1 + 0.06)^4$$
$$= 1,000 \ (1.06)(1.06)(1.06)(1.06)$$
$$= 1,000 \ (1.26248)$$
$$= 1,262.48.$$

The accumulated value of 1, regardless of the compounding method used, is a series of interest earnings (or payments) based on a single initial deposit. This idea is shown most graphically on a time chart like the one in Figure 1.5.

Using the example of monthly compounding over four months, the symbols on the graph can be translated into dollar amounts:

MONTH	6% INTEREST	BALANCE
		1,000.00
1	5.00	1,005.00
2	5.02	1,010.02
3	5.05	1,015.07
4	5.08	1,020.15

$$\text{where } AV = 1,020.15,$$
$$D = 1,000.00,$$
$$n = 1, 2, 3, 4 \text{ (months)},$$
$$i = 5.00, 5.02, 5.05, 5.08.$$

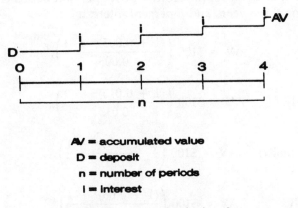

AV = accumulated value

D = deposit

n = number of periods

I = interest

FIGURE 1.5   Accumulated value of 1.

Accumulated Value of 1 Per Period

The accumulated value of 1 is the formula to use when you plan to invest a sum of money and leave it intact for an extended period of time. However, a new complication is added when you plan to make a series of regular deposits.

Example: You want to calculate the accumulated value that will be earned by depositing $100 per period, for a number of years, assuming both an interest rate and a compounding method.

The assumed question in this case is:

What will a series of deposits be worth after n periods, assuming r interest?

The formula for the accumulated value of 1 per period is expressed as:

Formula: Accumulated Value of 1 per Period

$$AV = D \left(\frac{(1 + r)^n - 1}{r} \right),$$

where
$$AV = \text{accumulated value,}$$
$$D = \text{deposits,}$$
$$n = \text{number of periods,}$$
$$r = \text{interest rate.}$$

The number of periods (n) and the interest rate (r) must be expressed in their appropriate forms. So for periodic deposits of $100, assuming three years and 6 percent interest:

Monthly: $AV = \$100 \left(\dfrac{(1 + 0.005)^{36} - 1}{0.005} \right);$

Quarterly: $AV = \$100 \left(\dfrac{(1 + 0.015)^{12} - 1}{0.015} \right);$

Semiannually: $AV = \$100 \left(\dfrac{(1 + 0.03)^6 - 1}{0.03} \right);$

Annually: $AV = \$100 \left(\dfrac{(1 + 0.06)^3 - 1}{0.06} \right).$

Another way this statement could be made is through the combination of single-deposit accumulations. On an annual basis, that would mean figuring out the interest on:

1. $100 for 3 periods;
2. $100 for 2 periods;
3. $100 for 1 period.

The three separate computations would then be added together. This becomes quite complex when interest must be figured for multiple periods. For example, monthly compounding over a three-year period would involve 36 separate steps.

The calculation assumes that a deposit will be made at the beginning of each period, and that interest will be accrued at the end of each period. Interest will be based on the previous period's ending balance. An example is shown in Figure 1.6.

To compute the accumulated value at the end of four periods, assuming $100 is deposited at the beginning of each month and compounding occurs monthly:

MONTH	DEPOSIT	6% INTEREST	BALANCE
1	100.00		100.00
2	100.00	.50	200.50
3	100.00	1.00	301.50
4	100.00	1.51	403.01

where AV = 403.01,
D = 100.00,
n = 1, 2, 3, 4 (months),
i = 0, .50, 1.00, 1.51.

Present Value of 1

The previous sections described the compounded growth of deposits or a series of deposits. The opposite problem is encountered when a target amount at the end of a period is known, and we need to determine the amount of deposit or deposits to make today.

Example: You want to accumulate a fund of $1,000 over a specified period of time, assuming a specified rate of interest. To calculate how much will be required in one single deposit today, you will apply the formula for the present value of 1.

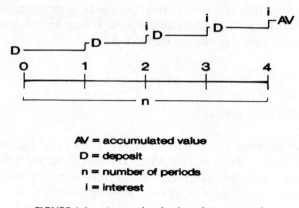

AV = accumulated value
D = deposit
n = number of periods
i = interest

FIGURE 1.6 Accumulated value of 1 per period.

The assumed question for this problem is:

How much must be deposited today to accumulate A target amount in n periods, assuming r interest?

In calculating accumulated value, the amount of the initial deposit was known. But for present value, the final value—the target amount—is known, and the required deposit is not. The formula for the present value of 1 is:

Formula: Present Value of 1

$$PV = \frac{1}{(1 + r)^n}$$

where
PV = present value,
n = number of periods,
r = interest rate.

If we assume that a fund of \$1,000 must be accumulated in four months, with monthly compounding at 6 percent, the formula is expressed as:

$$PV = 1,000 \left(\frac{1}{(1 + 0.005)^4} \right)$$
$$= 1,000 \left(\frac{1}{(1.005)(1.005)(1.005)(1.005)} \right)$$

$$= 1,000 \left(\frac{1}{1.02015}\right)$$
$$= 1,000 \ (0.98025)$$
$$= 980.25.$$

The present value calculation is shown in Figure 1.7.

We have established by formula that the present value of $1,000, over four months, and with 6 percent interest compounded monthly, is $980.25. The following table proves the formula:

MONTH	6% INTEREST	BALANCE
		980.25
1	4.90	985.15
2	4.93	990.08
3	4.95	995.03
4	4.97	1,000.00

To summarize,

$$A = 1,000.00,$$
$$PV = 980.25,$$
$$n = 1, 2, 3, 4 \text{ (months)},$$
$$i = 4.90, 4.93, 4.95, 4.97.$$

Sinking Fund Payments

The present value of 1 defines an amount of money that must be deposited at the beginning of a period in order to reach a target amount. When a

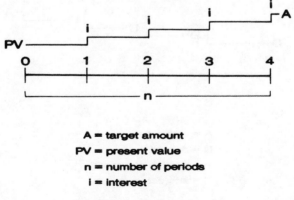

A = target amount
PV = present value
n = number of periods
i = interest

FIGURE 1.7 Present value of 1.

series of payments will be made, they are known as sinking fund payments. For this calculation, the assumed question is:

What amount of deposits must be made over n periods, assuming r interest, to accumulate A target amount?

The formula for sinking fund payments involves dividing 1 by the accumulated value of 1 for the number of periods involved, and at the same interest rate in effect.

Formula: Sinking Fund Payments

$$D = A \left[\frac{1}{((1 + r)^n - 1) / r} \right],$$

where

A = target amount,
D = deposits,
r = interest rate,
n = number of periods.

The series of required deposits, plus interest, will equal the target amount. This is illustrated in Figure 1.8.

The required sinking fund payment is the result of dividing '1' by the accumulated value of 1 per period for the same interest rate and compounding method. So to compute sinking fund payments to accumulate $1,000 in four months, it is first necessary to calculate the accumulated value of 1 per period, and then to insert the result into the formula:

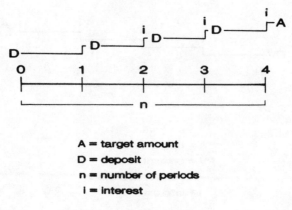

A = target amount
D = deposit
n = number of periods
i = interest

FIGURE 1.8   Sinking fund payments.

Step 1: Accumulated Value of 1 per Period

Month	AV of 1	
1	1	= 1.00000
2	1 + (1.005)	= 2.00500
3	1 + ((2.005) (1.005))	= 3.01500
4	1 + ((3.015) (1.005))	= 4.03008

Step 2: Formula for Sinking Fund Payments

$$D = 1,000 \frac{1}{((1 + 0.005)^4 - 1) / 0.005}$$

$$= 1,000 \left(\frac{1}{4.03008} \right)$$

$$= 1,000 (0.248134)$$

$$= 248.13.$$

To prove this calculation, apply it to the question, "How much must be deposited at the end of each of four months, to accumulate a fund of $1,000, assuming 6 percent interest compounded monthly?"

Answer:

		6%	
MONTH	DEPOSIT	INTEREST	BALANCE
1	248.13	0	248.13
2	248.13	1.24	497.50
3	248.13	2.49	748.12
4	248.13	3.74	999.99

$$\text{where } A = 1,000.00,$$
$$D = 248.13,$$
$$n = 1, 2, 3, 4 \text{ (months)},$$
$$i = 0, 1.24, 2.49, 3.74.$$

Present Value of 1 per Period

Another situation that requires computing the time value of money involves identifying a deposit required to fund a series of future withdrawals. The amount of each withdrawal, the time period, interest rate, and compounding method must all be taken into account.

The present value of 1 per period is used for retirement calculations and similar problems. For example, an investor purchases an annuity that will produce a regular monthly withdrawal for a specified number of years.

The calculation can also be used to determine a deposit required to make payments on a debt, or to produce short-term cash for other obligations.

Example: You plan to invest $1,000 per month for the next four months in a mutual fund account. Assuming that a savings account earns 6 percent, compounded monthly, how much must you have on deposit at the beginning of the four-month period, in order to meet your goal?

The assumed question for this problem is:

How much must be on deposit today to fund W withdrawals for n periods, assuming r interest?

The present value of 1 per period consists of the accumulation of factors for the present value of 1 (described earlier in this chapter). So the formula is made up of a series of additions:

Formula: Present Value of 1 per Period

$$PV = W\left[\left(1 - \frac{1}{(1 + r)^n}\right) / r\right],$$

where

$$
\begin{aligned}
PVl &= \text{present value,} \\
W &= \text{withdrawal amount,} \\
n &= \text{number of periods,} \\
r &= \text{interest rate.}
\end{aligned}
$$

Remember that the purpose of breaking down the formula is to identify the amount of initial deposit, as illustrated in Figure 1.9.

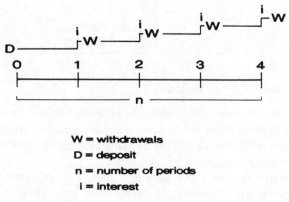

W = withdrawals
D = deposit
n = number of periods
i = interest

FIGURE 1.9   Present value of 1 per period.

Example: If we assume that payments of $1,000 must be made in each of four months, with monthly compounding at 6 percent, the formula can be developed as a series of calculations for the present value of 1, explained in these steps:

$$PV = 1,000 \left(1 - \frac{1}{(1.005)^4}\right)/0.005$$

$$= 1,000 \left(1 - \frac{1}{1.0201505}\right)/0.005$$

$$= 1,000 \ (1 - 0.9802475)/0.005$$

$$= 1,000 \left(\frac{0.0197525}{0.005}\right)$$

$$= 1,000 \ (3.95050)$$

$$= 3,950.50.$$

This calculation can be proved by adding interest for each month, and subtracting the planned withdrawal for each month. If the initial deposit, developed by figuring a series of present values of 1, is correct, the balance of the account at the end of four months will be zero:

MONTH	6% INTEREST	WITHDRAWALS	BALANCE
			3,950.50
1	19.75	1,000.00	2,970.25
2	14.85	1,000.00	1,985.10
3	9.93	1,000.00	995.03
4	4.97	1,000.00	0

where W = 1,000.00,
D = 3,950.50,
n = 1, 2, 3, 4 (months),
i = 19.75, 14.85, 9.93, 4.97.

Amortization Payments

The sixth calculation of interest involves determining a periodic payment required to retire a debt, such as a home mortgage or other loan. This assumes a specified time period, the amount of debt, and the rate of interest.

Example: You contract for a short-term loan in the amount of $4,000, payable in four equal monthly installments. Interest will be charged at the rate of 6 percent per year, compounded monthly. Thus, the monthly rate will be one-half of one percent.

The assumed question is:

> What amount of equal periodic payments must be made to retire a debt, over n periods, assuming r interest?

Without using an amortization table, the monthly payment can be computed if you already know the present value of 1 per period. We will use the amounts developed in the previous section to illustrate the point.

Formula: Amortization Payments

$$P = B\left(\frac{1}{PV^n}\right),$$

where

P = payment,
B = balance,
n = number of periods,
PV = present value of 1 per period.

Note: This formula is simplified in the sense that you need only the latest factor in a series of factors for the present value of 1 per period. In addition, there is no mention of the interest rate in the formula, since the appropriate present value factors would be used. The calculation of amortization payments is shown in Figure 1.10.

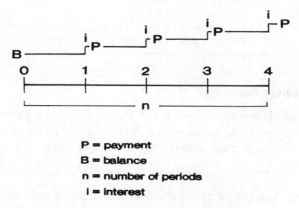

P = payment
B = balance
n = number of periods
i = interest

FIGURE 1.10 Amortization payments.

This calculation is proved in application to a short-term situation.

Example: A debt of $4,000 is to be retired in four equal monthly payments, with monthly compounding at 6 percent. Referring to the calculations for the present value of 1 per period and converting those money amounts to factors per 1, we can find the needed multiplier. Thus, the factor for the fourth month consists of the sum of factors for months one, two, three, and four:

Step 1: Find the Present Value Amounts:

	Present
Month	Value
1	995.02
2	990.08
3	985.15
4	980.25

Step 2: Add the Present Value Amounts:

995.02 + 990.08 + 985.15 + 980.25 = 3,950.50.

(*Note*: This value is the same as the present value of 1 developed in the previous section, for the fourth month.)

Step 3: Convert the Amount to a Factor:

The 3,950.50 shown above is a dollar amount. Since it is necessary to determine a factor *per 1*, this must be translated into a factor value. Because the amount is for the present value in thousands, the decimal place must be moved three places to the left:

Amount	to	Factor
3,950.50	=	3.95050

Step 4: Divide 1 by the Factor:

$$\frac{1}{3.95050} = 0.253133.$$

Step 5: Multiply the Factor by the Balance:

0.253133 × 4,000 = 1,012.53.

This process establishes that four monthly payments of $1,012.53 will retire the debt. This can be proved by multiplying the balance by one-half of one percent (6 percent, compounded monthly) to determine monthly interest; subtracting interest from the monthly payment to determine the principal payment; and then subtracting the principal from the balance:

Formula: Proof of Amortization Payments

1. Balance × periodic rate = interest;
2. Payment − interest   = principal;
3. Balance − principal   = new balance.

To apply this formula, using the required monthly payment developed above:

MONTH	PAYMENT	INTEREST	PRINCIPAL	BALANCE
				4,000.00
1	1,012.53	20.00	992.53	3,007.47
2	1,012.53	15.04	997.49	2,009.98
3	1,012.53	10.05	1,002.48	1,007.50
4	1,012.53	5.04	1,007.49	0.01

$$\text{where } B = 4{,}000.00,$$
$$P = 1{,}012.53,$$
$$n = 1, 2, 3, 4 \text{ (months)},$$
$$i = 20.00, 15.04, 10.05, 5.04.$$

Understanding how various formulas are developed and applied is an important step in the comprehension and mastery of the time value of money. So for any investor interested in gaining comfort with the use of tables and computation of present and future value, this is a worthwhile exercise.

As we pointed out in the beginning of this chapter, it is impractical to compute these formulas by hand. For short-term examples, a concept can be proved; but in many investment situations, you will be required to figure time value for more extended periods. The six tables that correspond to the computations described in this chapter are convenient tools to help you avoid having to compute long-term future and present values by hand. The next chapter explains how each table serves your purposes, and how you can build your own compound interest tables.

2

Mastering Interest Tables

The last chapter demonstrated how the time value of money is calculated for investment decisions. For short-term calculations, it is a simple matter to figure future or present value by hand; this idea is made clear by going through the manual steps involved.

Realistically, most investors must be concerned with time periods much greater than a few months or years. Thus compound interest tables are a necessary and valuable tool. These tables show the factor for extended time periods for a single dollar, enabling you to quickly determine values for any amount.

In this chapter, you will see how each of the six types of compound interest functions work and how tables are constructed and used. You will also learn how to estimate a factor through interpolation and how to build your own compound interest tables.

THE FACTOR

Interest tables show a series of factors for a specific value, but only for the value of one dollar. Tables are set up in this way because the *amount* is the greatest variable in the computation. So, when using tables, you must add that variable to arrive at your answer. If you required a table for every possible amount, the volume of tables would be endless, expensive to produce, and impractical.

You must have four types of information in order to use a compound interest table:

1. Interest Rate

The rate as stated is called the nominal rate. That's the annual percent of interest. However, in addition to knowing the nominal rate, you must also determine the compounding method to be used.

For example, a mutual fund might have yielded average annual returns of 15 percent per year. That's the nominal rate, regardless of whether interest was compounded monthly, quarterly, semiannually, or annually.

2. Time

How long a period must be calculated? You must know the time period in order to arrive at an answer to your question.

Remember that the time and the rate, together, are the critical factors in determining the present or future value of money. If you plan to leave a deposit in an account for three years, interest will compound modestly. If it's left there for 25 years, the effect of compounding will be much greater.

3. Amount

You must have an amount in mind, since the factors shown on the tables are for one dollar only. So when a table has the heading "accumulated value of 1," that means the reported factors are the compounded values of one dollar.

4. Specific Table

There are six different tables, each for a different calculation. This is the point at which many investors become discouraged. Each of the tables appears to be so similar that making a clear distinction is difficult. So, before using a compound interest table, it is essential that you comprehend its purpose.

Each table identifies the elements you need to make your calculation. The interest rate and compound method are listed at the top, and most books of tables are broken into four sections, one for each of the compounding methods. The time, in months and years, is shown in the first column; the table name appears above the factors.

With three of the four needed types of information supplied on the table, it is only necessary to locate the appropriate factor and then multiply it by the amount. The following example is the table for the accumulated value of 1.

Accumulated Value of 1

The first table reports factors to compute the accumulated value of 1 (dollar). This table shows how a single deposit, made at the beginning of a period of time, will grow.

Example: You deposit $5,000 in a mutual fund account and assume that it will earn an average of 12 percent per year, compounded

TABLE 1   Accumulated Value of 1 Dollar   **ANNUAL**

YEARS	11% NOMINAL ANNUAL RATE	11.5% NOMINAL ANNUAL RATE	12% NOMINAL ANNUAL RATE	12.5% NOMINAL ANNUAL RATE
1	1.110000	1.115000	1.120000	1.125000
2	1.232100	1.243225	1.254400	1.265625
3	1.367631	1.386196	1.404928	1.423828
4	1.518070	1.545608	1.573519	1.601807
5	1.685058	1.723353	1.762342	1.802032
6	1.870415	1.921539	1.973823	2.027287
7	2.076160	2.142516	2.210681	2.280697
8	2.304538	2.388905	2.475963	2.565785
9	2.558037	2.663629	2.773079	2.886508
10	2.839421	2.969947	3.105848	3.247321
11	3.151757	3.311491	3.478550	3.653236
12	3.498451	3.692312	3.895976	4.109891
13	3.883280	4.116928	4.363493	4.623627
14	4.310441	4.590375	4.887112	5.201580
15	4.784589	5.118268	5.473566	5.851778
16	5.310894	5.706869	6.130394	6.583250
17	5.895093	6.363159	6.866041	7.406156
18	6.543553	7.094922	7.689966	8.331926
19	7.263344	7.910838	8.612762	9.373417
20	8.062312	8.820584	9.646293	10.545094

annually. You want to know how much your account will be worth in 20 years.

Check the sample table above to find the answer. First, be sure it is the correct table. It is identified as a table for the "Accumulated value of 1 dollar with interest." It also tells you that compounding is annual. On this particular page, factors for 12 percent are included in the third factor column. The last line is the factor for 20 years, listed as 9.646293. When this factor is multiplied by the amount of your deposit, the answer is:

$$9.646293 \times \$5,000 = \$48,231.47.$$

If your assumption of a 12 percent annual growth rate is correct, a $5,000 deposit made today will grow to a value of $48,231.47 in 20 years.

Using a book of compound interest tables makes long-term interest calculations simple, by eliminating the need for a number of steps. But even with tables widely available, you might need to build your own tables in some instances. Most tables are broken down by half-percent rates only—6, 6.5, 7, and 7.5, for example. What if you need to know the factor for 7.25 percent? If you want to build your own table for the accumulated value of 1, you must use the correct formula, which is shown in Figure 2.1.

The formula for Table 1 states that the accumulated value of 1 is equal to 1 plus the interest rate, raised to the power of the number of periods involved. The interest rate, of course, must be adjusted according to the compounding method. So 12 percent remains 12 percent with annual compounding, and:

$$\begin{aligned}
\text{Semiannually} &= 6 \text{ percent;} \\
\text{Quarterly} &= 3 \text{ percent;} \\
\text{Monthly} &= 1 \text{ percent.}
\end{aligned}$$

To prove the table factors, apply the formula. For 12 percent interest with annual compounding, the first year's factor is listed as 1.120000. That factor, multiplied by 1.12, produces the second year's factor:

$$1.120000 \times 1.12 = 1.254400.$$

This step can be carried out for as many years as needed.

On a hand calculator this is a simple procedure:

Procedure: Hand Calculator Computation

   1. Enter 1.12.
   2. Press ×.
   3. Press = (for the second period).
   4. Press = (for each subsequent period).

$$AV = (1 + r)^n$$

AV = accumulated value of 1
r = interest rate
n = number of periods

FIGURE 2.1   Table 1 formula: Accumulated value of 1.

By pressing the = button 19 times (after steps 1 and 2), you will arrive at the factor for the twentieth year, with annual compounding. Your answer may be slightly different from the factor shown on the table, due to rounding. However, this will not create a problem in most instances, since the difference will normally be less than three ten-thousands of one cent. Going through the steps above on most hand calculators will produce a factor of 9.646291 rather than the correct factor of 9.646293.

Accumulated Value of 1 per Period

Closely related to Table 1 is the accumulated value of 1 per period, the factors in the second type of compound interest table. This table reports factors for compound interest for a series of deposits made at the beginning of each period.

Example: You plan to deposit $100 per month in a savings account. Your bank pays 6 percent and compounds interest monthly. You want to know what your account will be worth in 10 years.

It is possible to calculate the value in this account by going through a series of accumulated value calculations, one for each deposit; but that would involve 120 steps. It makes more sense to use Table 2, the formula for which is shown in Figure 2.2.

This formula states that the accumulated value of 1 per period is equal to 1, plus the previous factor times 1 plus the interest rate. To build Table 2, you must add a series of factors and then apply the interest rate to them. The following example is the table for the accumulated value of 1 per period.

Example: You deposit $100 per month in an account paying 6 percent interest, compounded monthly. That means that each month's interest will equal one-twelfth of the 6 percent nominal rate, or

$$AVP = 1 + (PF (1 + r))$$

AVP = accumulated value of 1 per period
PF = previous factor
r = interest rate

FIGURE 2.2 Table 2 formula: Accumulated value of 1 per period.

TABLE 2   Accumulated Value of 1 Dollar per Period
with Interest   **MONTHLY**

YEARS	5% NOMINAL ANNUAL RATE	5.5% NOMINAL ANNUAL RATE	6% NOMINAL ANNUAL RATE	6.5% NOMINAL ANNUAL RATE
1	12.278855	12.307170	12.335562	12.364034
2	25.185921	25.308560	25.431955	25.556111
3	38.753336	39.043331	39.336105	39.631685
4	53.014885	53.552852	54.097832	54.649927
5	68.006083	68.880823	69.770031	70.673968
6	83.764259	85.073412	86.408856	87.771168
7	100.328659	102.179391	104.073927	106.013400
8	117.740512	120.250282	122.828542	125.477348
9	136.043196	139.340512	142.739900	146.244833
10	155.282279	159.507582	163.879347	168.403154
11	175.505671	180.812233	186.322629	192.045460
12	196.763730	203.318634	210.150163	217.271134
13	219.109391	227.094572	235.447328	244.186218
14	242.598299	252.211661	262.304766	272.903856
15	267.288944	278.745550	290.818712	303.544767
16	293.242809	306.776160	321.091337	336.237756
17	320.524523	336.387916	353.231110	371.120256
18	349.202021	367.670008	387.353194	408.338901
19	379.346715	400.716657	423.579854	448.050147
20	411.033669	435.627395	462.040895	490.420930

0.005. The factor for the first month is 1.000000 (interest is calculated and added at the *end* of each period). The second month is computed by adding the previous factor, multiplied by the interest rate:

$$
\begin{aligned}
AVP &= 1 + (PF\,(1 + r)) \\
&= 1 + (1\,(1 + 0.005)) \\
&= 1 + (1\,(1.005)) \\
&= 1 + 1.005 \\
&= 2.005000.
\end{aligned}
$$

The factor for the second month is 2.005000. To figure out the value of depositing $100 per month, multiply the factor times the monthly deposit:

$$2.005000 \times 100 = \$200.50.$$

The same steps can be used to build a compound interest table at any rate of interest. While a book of tables is helpful as long as it lists rates that meet your situation, you often will need to figure out rates that lie between those shown on the tables.

Example: Your book of compound interest tables shows factors for monthly compounding at every half-percent. However, the account you recently opened pays interest at the rate of 6.75 percent. To build your own table:

1. Compute the monthly rate, based on the nominal rate of 6.75 percent:

$$\frac{0.0675}{12} = 0.005625.$$

2. Apply the formula for Table 2:

$$AVP = 1 + (PF (1 + r)).$$

3. Compute the table for the periods required: In this example, the first month's factor would be 1.000000, so the second month should be:

$$
\begin{aligned}
AVP &= 1 + (PF (1 + r)) \\
&= 1 + (1 (1 + 0.005625)) \\
&= 1 + (1.005625) \\
&= 2.005625.
\end{aligned}
$$

After two months, deposits of $100 would be worth:

$$2.005625 \times \$100 = \$200.56.$$

Present Value of 1

Table 3 reports factors for the present value of 1, which is the opposite of accumulated value. The following example is the table for the present value of 1. In this instance, you need to know how much to deposit today in order to accumulate a known target amount in a specified time period. The formula for this is shown in Figure 2.3.

This formula states that the present value of 1 (dollar) is equal to 1, divided by 1 plus the interest rate, raised to the power of the number of periods.

TABLE 3   Present Value of 1 Dollar   **ANNUAL**

YEARS	11% NOMINAL ANNUAL RATE	11.5% NOMINAL ANNUAL RATE	12% NOMINAL ANNUAL RATE	12.5% NOMINAL ANNUAL RATE
1	0.900901	0.896861	0.892857	0.888889
2	0.811622	0.804360	0.797194	0.790123
3	0.731191	0.721399	0.711780	0.702332
4	0.658731	0.646994	0.635518	0.624295
5	0.593451	0.580264	0.567427	0.554929
6	0.534641	0.520416	0.506631	0.493270
7	0.481659	0.466741	0.452349	0.438662
8	0.433926	0.418602	0.403883	0.389744
9	0.390925	0.375428	0.360610	0.346439
10	0.352184	0.336706	0.321973	0.307946
11	0.317283	0.301979	0.287476	0.273730
12	0.285841	0.270833	0.256675	0.243315
13	0.257514	0.242900	0.229174	0.216280
14	0.231995	0.217847	0.204620	0.192249
15	0.209004	0.195379	0.182696	0.170888
16	0.188292	0.175227	0.163122	0.151901
17	0.169633	0.157155	0.145644	0.135023
18	0.152822	0.140946	0.130040	0.120020
19	0.137678	0.126409	0.116107	0.106685
20	0.124034	0.113371	0.103667	0.094831

$$PV = \left(\frac{1}{1+r} \right)^n$$

PV = present value of 1
r = interest rate
n = number of periods

FIGURE 2.3   Table 3 formula: Present value of 1.

Example: You want to accumulate a fund worth $5,000 at the end of five years. You will place funds in a mutual fund account, on the assumption that you will earn an average of 12 percent per year, compounded annually. By checking an annual compounding table for 12 percent, you discover a factor of 0.567427. The amount required today is:

$$0.567427 \times \$5,000 = \$2,837.14.$$

You can prove the accuracy of this factor in two ways. First, recognizing that present and accumulated value are opposites, you can apply the accumulated value of 1 factor to the amount above. That table reports a five-year factor of 1.762342. Multiply that by the derived present value factor:

$$1.762342 \times \$2,837.14 = \$5,000.01.$$

Second, you can add 12 percent per year to the amount derived from the table:

YEAR	INTEREST	TOTAL
		2,837.14
1	340.45	3,177.59
2	381.31	3,558.90
3	427.07	3,985.97
4	478.32	4,464.29
5	535.71	5,000.00

Computation of each factor involves dividing 1 by the periodic interest rate. So if your calculation is for 12.25 percent and there is no table for that rate, the factor can be derived by applying the formula:

$$PV = \left(\frac{1}{1 + 0.1225} \right).$$

This formula is carried forward for five periods:

$$
\begin{aligned}
PV &= 0.890869 \text{ (first year)} \\
&= 0.793648 \text{ (second year)} \\
&= 0.707036 \text{ (third year)} \\
&= 0.629876 \text{ (fourth year)} \\
&= 0.561137 \text{ (fifth year)}.
\end{aligned}
$$

To reach the target of $5,000 in five years:

$$0.561137 \times \$5,000 = \$2,805.68.$$

Double-check the factor in use by hand-calculating, or by applying the factor for the accumulated value of 1 to the factor you develop for present value.

Sinking Fund Payments

Table 4 provides factors needed to compute periodic deposits required to meet your target amount. For example, you want to accumulate a fund worth $5,000 at the end of five years, with interest compounded annually. How much should you deposit at the beginning of each year? The following example is the table for sinking fund payments. The formula for sinking fund payments is shown in Figure 2.4.

TABLE 4   Sinking Fund Payments   **ANNUAL**

YEARS	11% NOMINAL ANNUAL RATE	11.5% NOMINAL ANNUAL RATE	12% NOMINAL ANNUAL RATE	12.5% NOMINAL ANNUAL RATE
1	1.000000	1.000000	1.000000	1.000000
2	0.473934	0.472813	0.471698	0.470588
3	0.299213	0.297776	0.296349	0.294931
4	0.212326	0.210774	0.209234	0.207708
5	0.160570	0.158982	0.157410	0.155854
6	0.126377	0.124791	0.123226	0.121680
7	0.102215	0.100655	0.099118	0.097603
8	0.084321	0.082799	0.081303	0.079832
9	0.070602	0.069126	0.067679	0.066260
10	0.059801	0.058377	0.056984	0.055622
11	0.051121	0.049751	0.048415	0.047112
12	0.044027	0.042714	0.041437	0.040194
13	0.038151	0.036895	0.035677	0.034496
14	0.033228	0.032030	0.030871	0.029751
15	0.029065	0.027924	0.026824	0.025764
16	0.025517	0.024432	0.023390	0.022388
17	0.022471	0.021443	0.020457	0.019512
18	0.019843	0.018868	0.017937	0.017049
19	0.017563	0.016641	0.015763	0.014928
20	0.015576	0.014705	0.013879	0.013096

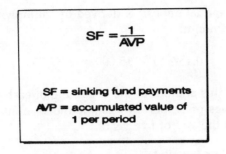

$$SF = \frac{1}{AVP}$$

SF = sinking fund payments
AVP = accumulated value of
1 per period

FIGURE 2.4   Table 4 formula: Sinking fund payments.

The formula states that sinking fund payments are equal to 1 divided by the accumulated value of 1 per period. So to develop a table for sinking fund payments, you need to first compute the accumulated value of 1 per period, and then divide 1 by the final factor.

Example: You want to build a fund worth $5,000 in five years, and you assume your mutual fund account will earn 12 percent per year, compounded annually. In order to develop the factor you need, refer to Table 2 (accumulated value of 1 per period), and divide 1 by the factor shown there:

$$SF = \frac{1}{AVP}.$$

The factor in Table 2 for five years is 6.352847. If no table is available, this can be computed by applying the formula for the accumulated value of 1, involving five calculations:

$$AVP = 1 + (PF (1 + r)).$$

Year	Factor
1	1.000000
2	2.120000
3	3.374400
4	4.779328
5	6.352847

Next, divide 1 by the five-year factor:

$$SF = \frac{1}{6.352847} = 0.157410.$$

The required annual deposit is derived by multiplying this factor by the target amount:

$$0.157410 \times \$5,000 = \$787.05.$$

By depositing this amount at the beginning of each year, and assuming earnings of 12 percent, compounded annually, you will have $5,000 at the end of five years.

Present Value of 1 per Period

Table 5 is a series of factors showing the amount of an initial deposit required to fund a series of regular payments.

Example: You recently purchased an interest in a limited partnership, which requires staged payments of $10,000 per year over a three-year period. How much must be deposited each year, assuming you will earn 12 percent compounded annually, to make each payment?

The answer is found by computing the present value of 1 per period. Referring to the 12 percent annual compounding table, you see that the factor is 2.401831. That factor is multiplied by the amount of each scheduled payment:

$$2.401831 \times \$10,000 = \$24,018.31.$$

Activity over a three-year period will be:

YEAR	INTEREST	WITHDRAWALS	BALANCE
			$24,018.31
1	$2,882.20	$10,000	16,900.51
2	2,028.06	10,000	8,928.57
3	1,071.43	10,000	0

The following example is the table for the present value of 1 per period. The formula for Table 5 is shown in Figure 2.5.

This formula states that the present value of 1 per period is equal to the addition of the present value factors, for the number of periods involved. Thus the table can be constructed from the computation of present values.

TABLE 5 Present Value of 1 Dollar per Period ANNUAL

YEARS	11% NOMINAL ANNUAL RATE	11.5% NOMINAL ANNUAL RATE	12% NOMINAL ANNUAL RATE	12.5% NOMINAL ANNUAL RATE
1	0.900901	0.896861	0.892857	0.888889
2	1.712523	1.701221	1.690051	1.679012
3	2.443715	2.422619	2.401831	2.381344
4	3.102446	3.069614	3.037349	3.005639
5	3.695897	3.649878	3.604776	3.560568
6	4.230538	4.170294	4.111407	4.053839
7	4.712196	4.637035	4.563757	4.492310
8	5.146123	5.055637	4.967640	4.882045
9	5.537048	5.431064	5.328250	5.228485
10	5.889232	5.767771	5.650223	5.536431
11	6.206515	6.069750	5.937699	5.810161
12	6.492356	6.340583	6.194374	6.053476
13	6.749870	6.583482	6.423548	6.269757
14	6.981865	6.801329	6.628168	6.462006
15	7.190870	6.996708	6.810864	6.632894
16	7.379162	7.171935	6.973986	6.784795
17	7.548794	7.329090	7.119630	6.919818
18	7.701617	7.470036	7.249670	7.039838
19	7.839294	7.596445	7.365777	7.146523
20	7.963328	7.709816	7.469444	7.241353

Example: You want to make periodic investments of $2,500 per year for the next five years and want to deposit a single sum today that will completely fund those investment payments. Your book of compound interest tables does not include the 12.25 percent assumed rate you expect to earn on your deposit. You can build your own table by computing a series of present value factors.

$$PVP = PV^1 + \ldots PV^n$$

PVP = present value of 1 per period
PV = present value of 1
n = number of periods

FIGURE 2.5 Table 5 formula: Present value of 1 per period.

Compute the present value of 1, assuming 12.25 percent interest, compounded annually:

$$PV = \frac{1}{1 + r}.$$

Year	PV of 1
1	0.890869
2	0.793648
3	0.707036
4	0.629876
5	0.561137

The present value of 1 per period after five years will consist of the addition of all five factors, or a total factor of 3.582566. You will need to deposit:

$$3.582566 \times \$2,500 = \$8,956.42.$$

To prove that this is the correct amount at 12.25 percent interest:

YEAR	INTEREST	WITHDRAWALS	BALANCE
			$8,956.42
1	$1,097.16	$2,500	7,553.58
2	925.31	2,500	5,978.89
3	732.41	2,500	4,211.30
4	515.88	2,500	2,227.18
5	272.83	2,500	0.01

Amortization Payments

Table 6, the last table, shows factors required to amortize an amount of money over time, given an assumed rate of interest. The best-known example of this type of payment is the one made on a mortgage.

Example: You invest $14,000 in a second mortgage, and the borrower agrees to make monthly payments to you over a five-year period. The agreed interest rate is 12 percent, compounded monthly. An amortization-payment table with these specifications will show a factor of 0.022244. Monthly payments required will be:

$$0.022244 \times \$14,000 = \$311.42.$$

Verification of the factor and amount would require 60 steps, one for each month in the five-year period. The following example is the table for amortization payments. The factor can also be proved by applying the formula for Table 6, shown in Figure 2.6.

This formula states that the amortization payment is equal to 1 divided by the present value of 1 per period. According to that table, the five-year factor for present value is 44.955038. Applying the formula for amortization payments, we have:

$$\frac{1}{44.955038} = 0.022244.$$

Developing your own tables for amortization payments will be more involved than for the other tables explained in this chapter, especially when compounding occurs on a monthly basis (the most common basis for pay-

TABLE 6   Amortization Payments   **MONTHLY**

YEARS	11% NOMINAL ANNUAL RATE	11.5% NOMINAL ANNUAL RATE	12% NOMINAL ANNUAL RATE	12.5% NOMINAL ANNUAL RATE
1	0.088382	0.088615	0.088849	0.089083
2	0.046608	0.046840	0.047073	0.047307
3	0.032739	0.032976	0.033214	0.033454
4	0.025846	0.026089	0.026334	0.026580
5	0.021742	0.021993	0.022244	0.022498
6	0.019034	0.019291	0.019550	0.019811
7	0.017122	0.017386	0.017653	0.017921
8	0.015708	0.015979	0.016253	0.016529
9	0.014626	0.014904	0.015184	0.015468
10	0.013775	0.014060	0.014347	0.014638
11	0.013092	0.013384	0.013678	0.013975
12	0.012536	0.012833	0.013134	0.013439
13	0.012075	0.012379	0.012687	0.012998
14	0.011691	0.012001	0.012314	0.012632
15	0.011366	0.011682	0.012002	0.012325
16	0.011090	0.011412	0.011737	0.012067
17	0.010854	0.011181	0.011512	0.011847
18	0.010650	0.010983	0.011320	0.011660
19	0.010475	0.010812	0.011154	0.011500
20	0.010322	0.010664	0.011011	0.011361

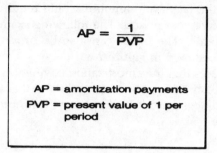

$$AP = \frac{1}{PVP}$$

AP = amortization payments
PVP = present value of 1 per
      period

FIGURE 2.6   Table 6 formula: Amortization payments.

ments of a debt). Because tables depend on factors developed in previous tables, this task would require three separate steps:

1. Develop factors for the present value of 1.
2. Add those factors to compute the present value of 1 per period.
3. Divide 1 by the final present value of 1 per period, to derive the factor for amortization payments.

For a five-year period, step 1 would require 60 separate computations. There is a faster method, not only for amortization payments, but for all six tables. That method is interpolation, the development of a close estimate of a factor.

INTERPOLATION

In most applications of the time value of money, a close estimate is adequate. This is especially true when you consider that in many cases, the entire exercise is based on assumption.

In estimating the value of your portfolio in 20 years, you may assume an average annual return. So many variables will affect the accuracy of your calculation that you do not need to depend on a precise factor. A close estimate will do.

Example: You lend money for a secured second mortgage at the rate of 12.25 percent. Your book of tables shows factors for 12 and 12.5 percent. To interpolate the monthly payment due, an estimate will be adequate, since the final payment can be adjusted for any amounts above or below the monthly payment.

3

Rates of Return

Investors constantly struggle with the problem of obscure or indefinite terminology. So many words and phrases are used in more than one context, that comparing investments to one another is not only dangerous—it is impossible without first understanding what "return" means in each case.

An example of the problem is found in the many uses of the words *return, yield,* and *profit.* All are applied to either a percentage or an amount earned on invested funds, on sales generated by a company, or on some other basis. In this chapter, we will explain the most common meanings of rates of return.

When you hear that a company earned 4.5 percent last year, what does that mean? Depending on the context, the statement could mean several things:

1. Profits were 4.5 percent of sales.
2. The stock's value rose 4.5 percent.
3. The dividend paid to shareholders was equal to 4.5 percent of the stock's market value.

Clearly, investors, stockbrokers, and others use many terms that require better definition. However, you cannot depend on any real clarification, except to the extent that it is built into required disclosure statements. And for that, you will have to read a prospectus or ask questions to find the real basis for comparison.

A second problem is that in many prospectuses, the basis for assumption, or the way that projections were developed, is not disclosed. By examining historical or projected results and challenging the underlying assumptions, you may discover that the basis for a claim is flawed.

The difficulty that all investors face in arriving at truly valid comparisons is aggravated by promoters and stockbrokers who use many terms interchangeably, without including clarification.

Example: Your stockbroker recommends two possible courses for your portfolio. First is the purchase of stock that is currently paying a 7 percent dividend; second is a bond that yields 7 percent interest. The broker remarks, "Both of these investments yield the same amount."

The comparison should not end there, although it often does. For the unwary investor, a complex decision is reduced to the simple comparison of a dividend rate and an interest rate, but, in fact, the risk factors in both stocks and bonds are quite complex. A true comparison cannot be made between the two, because the degree of risk in each dictates that your perception of "7 percent" must vary.

For the stock purchaser, there is the risk of uncertain future market value and, in some instances, the solvency of the company. And the board of directors may increase, decrease, suspend, or miss a dividend payment next quarter.

For the bond investor, 7 percent must be evaluated in light of the current premium or discount from the face amount. Risks also include the future rise or fall in market interest rates, which will affect the bond's market value *and* your perception of the rate. The decision must also be evaluated based on time to maturity and the rating of the company.

Every investor must develop some basis for decisions about buying and selling, and the timing of those actions. A valid comparison must temper the comparison of return (or potential for return) with an understanding of varying risk factors. This demands a comprehension of what a return constitutes and how it was computed; otherwise, the comparison cannot be an informed one. A good place to start is by defining some of the commonly used terms.

TYPES OF RETURN

One danger in attempting to compare investments is that the commonly used words often have different meanings. As a general rule, "yield" refers to dividends and interest earned on an investment. However, yield is also used to describe cash flow, dollar amount, and the percentage earned on a company's sales.

"Current yield" is a reference to the percentage being earned today, which may vary from the stated, or "nominal" yield. This is particularly applicable in the bond market. The nominal yield is the contractual percentage paid by the issuer, always as a percentage of the bond's face (maturity) value. However, the current yield will vary based upon the current market value of the bond. When the market value is higher than face value (or, at a premium), current yield is lower than nominal yield; and when the market value is lower than face value (or, at a discount), current value is higher. These variances are explained later in this chapter.

In any comparison of rates of return, you must be careful to ensure that two or more stated rates are based on the same premise. All too often, a current yield is, in error, compared to an annual yield; or the yield from annual dividends is mistakenly compared to historical price increases in the stock.

In addition to ensuring that the meaning of the return is identical for two unlike investments, you must also determine that the time period is the same. Two investments, each yielding 10 percent, may actually produce different dollar amounts when the holding period is not identical.

Example: One investment is held for 14 months and another for only 7 months. In both cases, investors increased their original investment by 10 percent. However, because the holding periods were not the same, the rates of return are not comparable. The solution is to compare both investments on the basis of annualized return.

To compute annualized return, divide the percentage of yield earned by the number of months held, and multiply the result by 12 (months):

Formula: Annualized Return

$$\frac{Y}{M} \times 12 = A,$$

where
$$Y = \text{yield,}$$
$$M = \text{months held,}$$
$$A = \text{annualized return.}$$

In the examples given, annualized returns for holding periods of 14 and 7 months are:

14 months:

$$\frac{10}{14} \times 12 = 8.57\%;$$

7 months:

$$\frac{10}{7} \times 12 = 17.14\%.$$

Because the same stated rate was earned in less time in the second example, the annualized rate is greater. This is the only dependable method for making investments with unlike periods truly comparable—to review them on the premise that a one-year holding period is a uniform measurement of yield. Whenever a return or yield is expressed without specifying otherwise, it is generally true that a one-year period is applicable.

This is certainly the rule for publicly listed companies, where the stock market investor is bombarded with numbers for net profits, earnings per share, sales, and a number of other fundamental tests. Unless a different period of time is specified, all of these fundamentals apply for one-year periods or averages.

The Income Statement

When you hear that a company earned 4.5 percent last year, the usual meaning is that profits were *that percentage of sales*. This is a popular measurement of a company's success, especially when compared to returns for previous years.

This comparison is commonly made by investors who track the fundamentals of companies, when seeking a viable stock investment. A growing organization may experience a series of gradual increases in net profits over time; others may be judged as successful when they are able to maintain the same level of profits during periods of sales expansion.

In either case, be cautious in comparing the quoted rates of return. There could be several different meanings.

The first caution point concerns one-time adjustments to reported profits, or what accountants call "extraordinary items." Examples include:

1. Changes in the method of valuing inventory.
2. Large profits or losses due to foreign-exchange rate fluctuations.
3. Capital gains or losses from the sale of assets.
4. Losses resulting from litigation or regulatory fines.
5. Write-off of obsolete or abandoned inventory or other assets.
6. Write-off of large uncollectible accounts receivable.
7. Casualty losses not covered by insurance.

If you are comparing two or more corporations with the intention of eventually purchasing stock in one, and if you consider net profits an important test, you must first ensure that the numbers you use are truly comparable. To achieve this, take these steps:

1. Adjust reported profits up or down by the amount of all extraordinary, nonrecurring items on the income statement.
2. Analyze not only the latest year, but the trend over three years or more. This information is supplied in annual reports or through research services like Value Line or Standard & Poor's.
3. Determine that "profit" means the same thing in each of the companies you compare.

You may be quoted the net operating profit, which excludes interest expense on the company's debt. In some cases, "profit" includes non-operating income such as a one-time capital gain from the sale of the company's headquarters building. And the reported profit might be what was earned without deducting a provision for federal income taxes.

Figure 3.1 summarizes the income statement format and the various forms of profit that might be reported in an annual statement or research report.

Gross profit is the amount earned after direct costs (material purchases, direct labor, and adjustments to inventory levels) are deducted from sales, but before any expenses are deducted. *Net operating profit* is a significant number, as it summarizes the results of the primary business for the year; however, it does not include federal income taxes.

The net operating profit is increased by other income (capital gains, interest income, and other sources of profits not related to operations); it is also reduced by other expenses (capital losses, interest expense, and other non-operating expenses). When a company is capitalized by excep-

total sales	$86,000,000	
cost of goods sold	53,415,000	
gross profit	$32,585,000	37.9%
operating expenses	27,104,000	
net operating profit	$5,481,000	6.4%
other income	419,000	
other expenses	(82,000)	
net pre–tax profit	$5,818,000	6.8%
federal income tax	1,978,000	
net after–tax profit	$3,840,000	4.5%

FIGURE 3.1 Income statement returns.

tionally high long-term debt, operating profits may be high, but a loss is reported—due to the burden of interest expenses. Other income and other expenses adjust operating profits to a net pre-tax level.

Federal income taxes are incurred whenever profits are reported, and can significantly reduce the amount of profit that actually goes to the bottom line. The rate of tax can vary, especially when a company is allowed to apply large losses from previous years, to reduce this year's tax burden.

The simple mathematical comparison of profits cannot stop at even a valid comparison of income statement results. For example, two similar organizations may operate quite differently in the area of dividend payments. This is not reflected on the income statement. One company earning 4.5 percent may pay out a large portion to stockholders each year; another may not declare a dividend at all. Depending on how significant a factor this is to you, it certainly must affect your comparison.

It is not always possible to compare two companies merely on the basis of net profits. For example, you are reviewing two publicly listed corporations, each of which reported about 4.5 percent net profits last year. However, in the first company's industry, 4.5 percent is considered relatively poor (when compared to the earnings of competitors); in the second company's industry, 4.5 percent is acceptable, or even far above expectations. So net profit return, by itself, is not necessarily a strong basis for comparison.

Just as investments held for different time periods cannot be accurately judged by the stated rate of return, a company's profits should always be compared for full years. If a new company is formed halfway through a year, its reported first-year results must be stated as a partial-year return. It should be understood that, given seasonal variances and a number of other factors, profits and sales for part-years are not necessarily reflective of what a company will do for the full year.

A company may break down its current earnings by part-years. For example, corporations issue quarterly reports showing the latest full year, followed by the latest fiscal quarter. In most cases, a comparison is made not to the previous full year, but to the same quarter for the previous fiscal year. That adjusts for seasonal factors, and enables investors to make intelligent comparisons.

In some forms of investment, net income is explained differently than on the traditional income statement. For example, income in real estate investments may be described as net net income, which refers to actual cash flow with all income and payments taken into account.

Example: In one real estate investment, the following results were reported as of the end of the year:

Gross Income	$128,000
Operating Expenses	42,300
Mortgage Interest	34,000
Mortgage Principal	49,200

Because principal payments are not deductible, the simple net profits for the year are $51,700, consisting of gross income less operating expenses and interest. But the net net income is only $2,500, representing the net income minus principal payments—or the cash flow from the investment.

RETURNS ON STOCK AND CAPITAL

Most investors are familiar with the standard net profit as widely reported in corporate financial statements, and excepting those special cases where cash flow is included in the adjustment. When a company's earnings rise, its stock often reflects the approval of the investing community. And when it falls, market prices fall as well, even when the future is promising.

Investors watch a number of other return indicators in their tracking of stocks, including the yield on common stock and the return on invested capital. Yield on common stock is also called the dividend yield. To compute this, divide the annual dividend per share by the current market price, as shown in Figure 3.2.

In this example, the yield on common stock equals 6.25 percent. A dividend of five dollars per share is declared, and market value is $80 per share. The actual yield changes each time the market price of the stock goes up or down. If market value falls to $75 per share, dividend yield will be 6.67 percent; and if the price rises to $85 per share, yield will fall to 5.88 percent.

For investors concerned with income from their stock investments, a comparison of dividend yields is certainly a critical test. It also adds an element for judgment when other factors are equal.

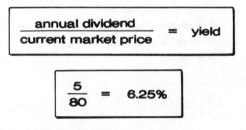

FIGURE 3.2   Yield on common stock.

A more involved ratio is called the return on invested capital. In cases where no long-term debt exists, this is computed by dividing net income by the average shareholders' equity for the year. The average equity is the weighted average of common stock.

Example: At the beginning of the year, a corporation's stock is valued at $34 million. At the end of the eighth month, an additional stock offering is made, and outstanding stock increases by $8 million, to $42 million. To determine the average, the stock must be weighted; for eight months (⅔ of the year), stock was worth $34 million, and for four months, it was valued at $42 million. The year's average value was $36.67 million.

This ratio becomes more complex when long-term debts are outstanding. Corporations that issue long-term bonds, for example, have two major sources of capitalization:

1. Stockholders' equity—the value of stock purchased in the corporation, or the equity interest.
2. Bondholders' debt—the value of bonds purchased by investors and owed by the corporation by contract, or the debt capitalization.

To compute the return on invested capital, you must recognize that "capital" includes both equity and debt. Thus, to the stockholder, profit is a return on an equity investment. And to the bondholder, the company's interest expense is also a form of return.

The formula for this ratio is shown in Figure 3.3.

$$\frac{N + I}{E + B} = R$$

N = net income
I = interest expense
E = shareholders' equity
B = par value of long-term bonds
R = return

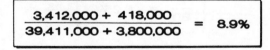

$$\frac{3,412,000 + 418,000}{39,411,000 + 3,800,000} = 8.9\%$$

FIGURE 3.3   Return on invested capital.

In this formula, net profits are added to the amount paid in interest expense. This calculation recognizes that profits and interest, together, represent forms of return on invested debt and equity capital. Even though interest expense (paid to bondholders) reduces net profits (retained earnings for stockholders), they belong together for the purpose of return on invested capital.

OPTION RETURNS

Special calculations for return are computed by those who invest or speculate in options. This is necessary because of the unusual nature of options, and the possible multiple sources of profits.

Options are contracts directly tied to price movement in an underlying stock. An investor who sells a call option promises to sell 100 shares of stock, at a specified price and by a specified date. If that date (the expiration date) passes and the option is not exercised, it expires. That will occur if the stock's price is lower than the exercise price. However, if the stock's price is higher than the exercise price, the option will be exercised. Upon exercise, the seller is required to deliver the 100 shares.

There are three possibilities for the option seller. First, the sold option may expire worthless. Second, the option may be exercised by the buyer. And third, the seller may cancel the position before expiration date (by buying the option, and thus cancelling the short position). In all three cases, the seller receives a premium (payment) at the time the option is sold.

These three possible outcomes will result in widely varying rates of return. The potential for loss must be included. Before an option player opens a position, the possible outcomes and risks should be calculated. The smart investor always evaluates not only the potential for profit, but the risk of loss as well.

If the seller does not own 100 shares of stock at the time an option is sold, the possible loss can be unlimited. For example, an investor sells one call option with a striking price of $40 per share. Before the expiration date, the stock rises to $65 per share and the option is exercised. The seller is forced to buy 100 shares at the market price of $65, and then to sell at the contracted price of $40. This unlimited loss makes uncovered option selling a very high-risk strategy.

A more conservative approach is to sell options only on stock owned by the seller. For example, you own 100 shares of XYZ Corporation, which you purchased at $48 per share. You sell an option with a striking price of $50 per share, and you receive a premium of $300 for selling the option. There are three potential sources of profit in this position:

1. *Capital gain* If the option is exercised by the buyer, you will gain $200 upon sale. The exercise price is $50, and your cost is $48 per share.

2. *Dividends* Even though you have promised to honor the option, you still own the stock as long as the option has not been exercised. Thus, you continue to earn dividends.

3. *Option premium* As a seller, you are paid a premium for selling.

There are three ways this transaction can turn out, all based on two variables. First is the price movement of the underlying stock. If the stock's value decreases or remains below the $50 strike price, the option will not be exercised. However, if the stock's price moves above the $50 level, the option may be exercised at any time before the expiration date.

The second variable is your own action. You may close the option position at any time by making an offsetting purchase. This action cancels the contract. If the stock's price has moved above the $50 strike price, the option's value will rise as well; and you will have to pay accordingly. However, if the stock's price remains below the $50 price, the option can be cancelled for a lower amount.

As the expiration date nears, options lose value rapidly. A portion of the premium cost is called time value, and that diminishes quickly toward the end of the option's cycle. By the expiration date, the only value left in an option contract is approximately equal to the intrinsic value. For example, if your stock is valued at $51 per share on expiration date, intrinsic value is 1 (dollar per share) and the option contract will be worth about $100 (each option contract is for one hundred shares).

The three possible returns from a covered call sale are:

1. *Return if exercised:* If the contract is exercised, you will be required to give up your stock at the exercise price of $50 per share. In our example, that translates to a $200 profit (before brokerage commissions), since your basis is $48 per share. In addition, you will have earned dividends. And you will keep the premium you received for selling the option.

2. *Return if unchanged:* If the stock's value remains below $50 per share, the option will not be exercised, but will expire worthless. In this case, you will have earned dividends and the call premium. However, you will also still own the 100 shares.

3. *Return if cancelled:* The third possibility is that you will cancel the position by buying the option. For example, the stock's value remains just below $50 per share, but the option declines in value to $100. You purchase, making a profit of $200 (sale of $300, minus purchase of $100). That, plus any dividends earned, is your profit.

Figure 3.4 shows these three outcomes, assuming that dividends of $120 were earned during the time the option contract was outstanding. The return-if-cancelled calculation assumes that the option's value decreased. However, a covered call seller may also close a position because the stock's value rose, resulting in a loss.

All three returns must be computed on the basis of the stock's purchase price. However, for the second and third calculations, you will still own the stock after the option position closes; thus, the calculation is an interim one only.

The returns as shown in the figure are:

> Return if exercised   12.90%;
> Return if unchanged   8.75%;
> Return if cancelled   6.67%.

An option will never exist for a cycle exceeding nine months. Thus, all of these returns should be compared on an annualized basis. For example, if these three outcomes occurred over a seven-month period, the annualized returns would be calculated using the formula for annualized return:

$$\frac{\text{return}}{12} \times \text{Months held} = \text{Annualized return.}$$

As an alternative to dividing the total rate, the amount earned can be divided by 12, and multiplied by the months held, to arrive at the average

	RETURN IF EXERCISED	RETURN IF UNCHANGED	RETURN IF CANCELLED
STOCK			
exercise value	5,000		
less: cost	4,800		
capital gain	200		
plus: dividends	120	120	120
OPTION			
sale	300	300	300
purchase			(100)
total return	$620	$420	$320

FIGURE 3.4 Option returns.

annual amount earned. That, divided by the original cost basis, results in the annualized return percentage.

The calculation of *return if exercised* is one form of another calculation, called total return. However, the total holding period must be taken into account to correctly compute the total return. As it applies to options, total return includes all sources of income: capital gain, dividends, and the premium. This return is then annualized and expressed as a rate for the entire period that the stock was owned.

Example: Refer to the return-if-exercised calculation; note that the option activity takes place during a seven-month period. However, the stock was purchased nine months before the option was sold. Thus, total return must be calculated for a 16-month holding period. This is illustrated in Figure 3.5.

Total return is also applied to non-option investments. For example, an investor in real estate will include a calculation of the difference in adjusted sale and purchase price; any rental income received; operating expenses paid; mortgage interest; depreciation on the property; and tax benefits.

Some applications of total return may include tax benefits, or may calculate the return on an after-tax basis. The return of $2,400 shown in Figure 3.5 would be reduced, either for an assumed tax rate or for the rate the investor actually pays during the year.

The total return calculation may also be taken a step farther, to allow

sale price	$5,840
purchase price	4,000
capital gain	$1,840
dividends	160
option premium	400
total return	$2,400

HOLDING PERIOD, 16 MONTHS:

$$\frac{\$2,400}{16} \quad \times \quad 12 \quad = \quad \$1,800$$

annualized
total return = 45.0%

FIGURE 3.5   Total return.

for inflation. In that case, the cash return would be reduced by both the tax rate and the inflation rate, usually based on the Consumer Price Index during the holding period. These additional adjustments of total return are valid only for the purpose of comparing unlike investments on a like basis.

Example: You earn $2,400 over a 16-month period from buying and selling stock and also selling a covered call. During an 11-month period, you also buy and sell 100 shares of another stock. To compare both investments on a thorough total-return basis, you compute the effect of taxes on each return, and also adjust profits downward for the applicable rate of inflation.

BOND YIELDS

Specialized calculations are applied to investments in bonds, due to the effects of discounts and premiums. The true return on bond investments is not limited to the stated nominal rate.

Example: You purchase a bond that pays 10 percent and has 11 years until maturity. As long as you buy the bond at face value, you will earn a 10 percent nominal yield each year. However, you may also purchase the bond at a premium (paying more than face value) or at a discount (paying less than face value).

Bond market values vary based on a comparison between the fixed interest rate of the bond and current interest rates. If you purchase a bond yielding 10 percent and market rates subsequently fall, you continue to receive 10 percent; and the market value of the bond will rise. But if rates exceed the fixed 10 percent rate, the market value of the bond will fall.

If you purchase a bond at a premium or discount, the difference between purchase price and face value is amortized or accrued over the remaining years until maturity, to adjust the actual yield earned each year. The resulting return is called *yield to maturity*. This may be expressed as the rate of return an investor can expect to earn on a bond that is held to maturity, on the assumption that all income earned will then be reinvested at the same rate being earned on the bond, adjusted for the difference between premium (or discount) and the face value of the bond.

Example: A bond pays a yield of 10 percent, and will mature in 11 years. If purchased at face value, the annual yield will be 10 percent. However, the yield is different if the bond is purchased at a premium or at a discount.

If the bond is purchased at 102, the yield must be calculated with that premium in mind. Rather than paying $10,000, an investor spends $10,200 when the price is at 102. The interest payments of $1,000 per year (10 percent of the face value) represent a different yield in this case:

$$\frac{1,000}{10,200} = 9.80\%.$$

If the bond is purchased at 98, or at a discount of $200, the annual yield is higher:

$$\frac{1,000}{9,800} = 10.2\%.$$

These calculations represent one version of yield to maturity. Because the investor pays an amount other than the bond's face value, the amount of interest received each year is stated precisely, with premium or discount in mind.

An alternative way that yield to maturity is described involves comparing bond yields to an alternate investment, based on the assumption that the alternate will pay the same rate of interest over the period of time until the bond's maturity. The comparison is often used to show the validity of investing in bonds; however, the comparison is not always valid.

For example, you may compare a bond investment to putting money in an insured savings account paying an identical yield. However, you have the choice of removing money from a savings account whenever you wish; with a bond, you cannot remove funds until maturity date unless you sell at current market value. Another flaw in the comparison is in the assumption that a savings rate will remain unchanged for the same period that the bond has not yet matured. This is not always the case.

Another bond calculation is called *yield-to-average-life*. This is the estimated yield that will be earned in a bond mutual fund, based on two assumptions: that the portfolio held at the time the yield is calculated will not change, and that all income will be reinvested.

This is a worthwhile calculation for judging different bond funds or for tracking the earning history of a single fund. However, it is not what an investor can realistically expect to earn. The bond fund's management must be expected to buy and sell bonds quite actively unless dealing with a fixed unit-investment trust rather than an open-end bond fund. In a unit-investment trust, a fixed portfolio of bonds is purchased and allowed to mature over time; that is not the case in a bond fund, where the portfolio may change quite frequently.

The yield-to-average-life is one means for evaluation of a fund's potential for long-term earnings, even when an investor understands that today's yield will not necessarily apply tomorrow.

In contrast, many bonds and related debt instruments are designed to yield a return in one year or less. The calculation of yield from a bond with less than a year to maturity must take into account both the discount and the adjustment in time. A common application of this is the calculation for discount yield. Some debt instruments issued by the federal government are always purchased at a discount and, rather than paying a stated yield, mature at face value. Treasury bills are auctioned for three-month, six-month, and one-year terms, and are always sold at a discount.

Example: A debt instrument with maturity value of $10,000 is purchased with a $200 discount and 75 days until maturity. The discount yield on this investment must calculate both the discount amount and the days until maturity.

The formula for discount yield is shown in Figure 3.6.

INTERNAL RATE OF RETURN

Some investments—notably limited partnerships—use a calculation known as the internal rate of return to estimate likely yields investors can earn. This is an especially complicated form of yield, because:

1. There are many ways that it is calculated, or many different calculations that are labeled internal rate of return.
2. The calculation involves the use of an assumed rate of interest that investors could earn in alternative investments. But because such a comparison does not take varying risks and liquidation periods into consideration, the assumption may be flawed.
3. Both income and expenses from an investment are estimated for the future. Thus, both the assumption about interest rates *and* the actual cash flow the investment will produce are subject to wide variances.

The only dependable way to use internal rate of return is to ignore the assumptions made by program sponsors, and apply your own set of assumptions to estimated income and expenses. For example, you may assume that, as a general rule, you expect to earn 8 percent (compounded annually) on your portfolio. With that in mind, you calculate the internal rate of return on several limited partnerships, using the estimated income and expenses as reported in the prospectuses.

Internal rate of return not only calculates the return on an initial investment, but also adjusts that return with the time value of money in mind. For example, a return of $1,000 on a $5,000 investment has a different time value over a five-year period than it has for a one-year period. This assumes that the income is reinvested at the assumed rate.

Example: A program requires an initial investment of $5,000, and the prospectus estimates net earnings of $6,750 over a five-year period. This is broken down on a schedule:

YEAR	EXPENSES	INCOME
1	$1,050	$ 0
2	400	0
3	400	800
4	0	800
5	0	7,000
Total	$1,850	$8,600
Net Income		$6,750

Other programs you also review estimate varying levels of income and expense over a similar period, usually with a final-year lump sum to come from selling appreciated properties. To make a valid comparison, you assume that you could earn 8 percent, compounded annually, as a general average.

To calculate internal rate of return, you must multiply each year's income or expense estimates by a present value factor. The factors

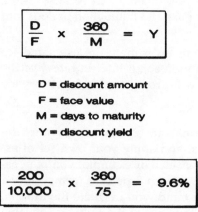

$$\frac{D}{F} \times \frac{360}{M} = Y$$

D = discount amount
F = face value
M = days to maturity
Y = discount yield

$$\frac{200}{10,000} \times \frac{360}{75} = 9.6\%$$

FIGURE 3.6   Discount yield.

$5,000 INVESTMENT, ASSUMING 8% RETURN:

YEAR	EXPENSES	INCOME	PRESENT VALUE FACTORS*	PRESENT VALUE
1	1,050	0	.925926	(972)
2	400	0	.857339	(343)
3	400	800	.793832	318
4	0	800	.735030	588
5	0	7,000	.680583	4,764
	$1,850	$8,600		
net		$6,750		$4,355
average per year				$ 871
annual return				17.4%

* present value based on annual compounding

FIGURE 3.7   Internal rate of return.

for 8 percent and annual compounding are used to multiply each program's estimates, to arrive at a comparable rate, as shown in Figure 3.7.

This is only one of several methods used to calculate internal rate of return. Many program sponsors have devised more complicated, elaborate ways to estimate this, but, given the problem that the entire matter is based on estimates and assumptions, it must be left to you to apply a comparable assumed rate and method of computation to actually compare one investment to another.

Example: You compare two different programs, each of which includes internal rate-of-return calculations in the prospectus. One assumes a rate of 8 percent and the other uses 11 percent. Comparing the two is not valid, because the assumptions about what you can earn outside of the investment, are not given at the same rate.

As complicated as it is to make yield, profit, and return comparable between unlike programs and investments, the key is identifying assumptions and estimates, and studying the prospectus or annual report; and then making certain that *your* comparisons are correct. Because so much investment literature is prepared with dissimilar assumptions and definitions of profit, it is not safe to believe the comparisons are all equally valid.

The true yield you earn is further affected by the variables of inflation and taxes. These factors in the investment decision have been misrepresented and distorted by many salespeople and program sponsors, often to the point that decisions have been made not on an intelligent, fact-based level, but in an attempt to counteract tax and inflation costs. The next chapter shows how economically sound investments can be selected with tax and inflation variables in mind, and how to make an evaluation using inflation and tax math.

4

Taxes and Inflation

The investment decision-making process might be a fairly simple one if taxes and inflation were not influencing factors. These two considerations add such a high degree of uncertainty to all investment questions that they often dominate. As a result, some decisions are made based not on the economic value of a company or management group, but for the hedging benefits and strategies built into a program.

This is a dilemma for you. In forecasting the future effects of taxes and inflation, you must depend on assumptions, and these are often flawed.

TAXES AS AN ECONOMIC FACTOR

As originally perceived and designed, income taxes were intended to fund the government's programs for the common good. However, the system has become so influential on the economy that federal taxing policy has itself become an economic factor.

For example, when the economy becomes recessionary, a change in the federal income tax law can and does have a direct effect on the recession. Provisions like the investment tax credit (which has been put into effect and later taken away several times), capital gains, favorable treatment of interest and dividend income, and rules for investment interest and passive losses, all determine the ways in which investors and corporations act.

We see a constant struggle between the need to increase federal revenues, and the need to encourage investment, both by businesses (in plant, equipment, and inventory) and in publicly traded company stock. When the tax rules favor investment, the economy grows strong; and when the rules take away those benefits, federal revenues increase but the economy suffers.

Admittedly, the question is a complex one. Because the income tax has such a strong and direct effect on our business and investment economy, even a moderate change in the rules may have a drastic effect. In the ideal free economy, income taxes would not play a major role in business de-

cisions; nor would they act as punitive measures against the most pro-
ductive members of society; nor would the viability of an investment be
affected by the rules for treatment of investment profits.

Taxation became exceptionally complicated during the 1980s, as anyone
who files a tax return already knows. Some of the facts:

- By 1986, approximately 40 percent of all individuals whose returns
  were prepared by someone else filed for extensions. Before that year,
  only 15 percent used the extension privilege.
- The tax bill introduced in 1981 was 185 pages. In 1984, the tax bill
  grew to 564 pages.
- The Tax Reform Act of 1986, once promoted as "simplification," took
  up 879 pages.
- The technical corrections bill, which was passed just to correct errors
  in the 1986 legislation, ran 960 pages.

What all of this means for investors is that the methods for determining
a profitable investment have become more complex. The estimate of future
tax liabilities—always one of the factors to consider in the investment
decision—is more complex now than ever before, for several reasons:

1. We have no way of knowing what future changes will be enacted.
   Between 1980 and 1986, new tax legislation averaged one new major
   bill per year.
2. Frequent changes can easily take today's popular investment out of
   favor tomorrow.
3. Computing an actual tax liability is so complex that outside help is
   needed by a growing number of people.

Rather than simplifying the investor's life, changes in the tax rules
have complicated it far beyond the complications of the past. Much of the
legislation we have seen recently was intended to close loopholes, but
chances are, those very changes have created more loopholes than ever.

THE MATH OF TAXES

In the past, many investment decisions could be made strictly for the tax
benefits they offered. Widespread abuses, especially in the limited partnership market, led to many of the reforms that have changed the meaning
of simplification.

Today, rather than evaluating an investment for its tax benefits, we
are faced with a bewildering and uncertain possibility. The tax conse-

quences of investing in the stock market, bonds, mutual funds, real estate, or any other market will be far more complicated than in the past. A successful investor may be subject to alternative minimum tax, passive loss limitations, or restrictions on deductibility of investment interest expense.

In the late 1970s, investments were evaluated by comparing future tax benefits or consequences. That can no longer be done, because of the uncertainty of future rules. In one respect, this is a positive change. Now, rather than making a decision motivated primarily by future taxation, we must select investments that offer the best possible economic outcome. That evaluation must be done on an after-tax basis, assuming the worst possible punitive effect from the tax rules.

During the late 1970s, investor activity in limited partnership programs was sparked by two factors. First was the steady growth in real estate values (and the majority of programs were in real estate investment). And second was the tax benefit of investment. It was possible in those days to make a profit just in tax savings. Individuals in the highest tax brackets were not concerned with ultimate profits from their investments, because they could save more in taxes than they invested in a program.

As tax reform progressed in the early 1980s, the promoters of real estate programs argued that "good" investments were made for the economics of a program and not just for tax benefits. This might still be true today; however, the traditional limited partnership form of investment has been forced to undergo radical changes, primarily due to continuing tax reform. Taxes and the related limitations on passive losses have made some forms of investment impractical.

We cannot escape the reality that our investment decisions will be affected by their tax consequences. And we must compare various alternatives with those consequences in mind.

Taxes and the Rate of Return

The amount of tax you will have to pay on investment profits will depend on the total of all taxable income you earn during the year. Tax is computed not on gross income, but on taxable income, which is the amount left over after reducing total earnings for deductions and exemptions.

The following illustration is based on rules in effect for the tax year 1988. The rules and rates may change in future years.

> *Example:* A married couple with three children earns gross income during the year of $50,000. A family may reduce its gross income by exemptions of $1,950 per person; and the standard deduction is $5,000. (If deductions, including mortgage interest, medical expenses, taxes, and contributions, exceed $5,000, you may choose to itemize; however, for the purpose of our example, we will assume that only the standard deduction is claimed.)

The taxable income for the year is computed by reducing gross income by exemptions and standard deduction:

Gross Income	$50,000
Exemptions ($1,950 × 5)	−9,750
Balance	$40,250
Standard Deduction	5,000
Taxable Income	$35,250

Reference to the tax tables will show that the total tax liability on this taxable income is $5,996. That represents 17 percent of taxable income and 12 percent of gross income.

To evaluate the effect of a profitable investment in this situation, it is first necessary to make the assumption that the profit would increase taxable income above the given level.

Example: Last year, your taxable income was $35,250, and you expect to earn the same amount this year. However, if you sell shares of stock and make a profit of $3,000, how will that affect your tax liability? Would it be realistic to multiply your profit by 17 percent? Or by 12 percent?

Because the tax rates are based on plateaus of income, you cannot use either percentage to compute the tax consequences of increasing income. You must first understand that the tax bracket will determine your final liability.

In the case of a married couple, the brackets for 1988 were:

TAXABLE INCOME RANGE	TAX RATE
$ 0 to $ 29,750	15%
$ 29,751 to $ 71,900	28%
$ 71,901 to $149,250	33%
$149,251 and above	28%

A married couple with $35,250 in taxable income pays tax in both the 15 percent and the 28 percent bracket. The first $29,750 is subject to the 15 percent rate:

$$\$29,750 \times 15\% = \$4,462.50.$$

The balance is taxed at the higher bracket, 28 percent. First, reduce total taxable income by the amount subject to the 15-percent bracket:

$$\$35,250 - \$29,750 = \$5,500.$$

Next, multiply the result by 28 percent:

$$\$5,500 \times 28\% = \$1,540.$$

When the two tax amounts are added together, the total liability is found:

15% bracket	$4,462.50
28% bracket	+1,540.00
Total Tax	$6,002.50

The small difference in this amount and the amount previously calculated results from the use of tax tables, where tax is computed in ranges of income.

With the different bracket amounts in mind, you must calculate your total tax liability at the rate of 28 percent. If you increase next year's taxable income with an investment profit of $3,000, your increased tax liability will be:

$$\$3,000 \times 28\% = \$840.$$

The estimate will be much different if you time your sale to occur in a year when income is lower. For example, during one year your total taxable income is estimated at $25,000. Since the 15 percent bracket extends up to $29,750, a sale during that year will result in additional tax at the rate of 15 percent:

$$\$3,000 \times 15\% = \$450.$$

Tax-deferred Profits

Whenever you are able to earn a profit without having to also pay taxes, the true after-tax profit is much higher. One of the favorite questions investment salespeople like to ask is, "Would you rather earn a profit that's taxable or one that's tax-free?"

Even though the answer is obvious, you are limited in the ways that profits may be deferred or exempted from taxes after tax reform. Even a tax-free yield may be taxed, if your profits and total income are high enough to be subjected to alternative minimum tax.

Some investment earnings can take place in tax-deferred situations. Examples include:

1. Certain annuities and life insurance investments designed for retirement.
2. Residential real estate, where profits are deferred if you buy a new home within a two-year period.
3. Individual Retirement Accounts (IRAs), in which all profits are deferred until the withdrawal date.
4. Keogh plans for the self-employed, which yield tax-deferred earnings and allow the individual to reduce gross income for all contributions to the plan.
5. Employer-sponsored profit-sharing and pension plans, which are not taxed until the distribution date.

A comparison of before-tax and after-tax yields shows that a substantial difference can result, especially after many years.

Example: You plan to deposit $100 per quarter in a mutual fund, to save for retirement in 25 years. The estimated earnings in this account will be 10 percent per year, compounded quarterly.

Your total effective tax rate today is estimated at 30 percent, representing combined federal and state tax rates. Thus, the after-tax yield will be approximately 70 percent of the total estimate, or 7 percent.

You may decide to make this investment through an Individual Retirement Account, where earnings will be deferred; or to open an account in your name, and pay the tax each year. With taxes in mind, the difference in 25 years will be:

Tax-deferred Account Value	$43,255
Taxable Account Value	$26,675
Difference	$16,580

The comparison is not perfect, because the tax you pay each year will not actually be deducted from your investment. You will pay the increased tax while leaving your deposit intact. In most cases, the account would still grow to its full 25-year value. However, the added amount of taxes must be paid separately each year. This illustration is useful for the purpose of comparison between taxable and tax-deferred investing, even though it does not truly indicate an account's value at the end of the period.

The before-tax and after-tax effects are illustrated in Figure 4.1.

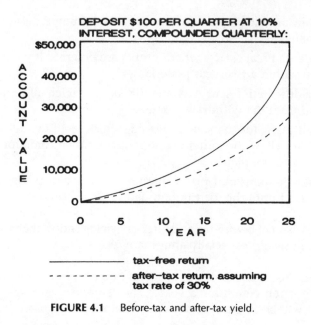

FIGURE 4.1   Before-tax and after-tax yield.

THE INFLATION FACTOR

While the tax issue adds an uncertain future consequence to your investment yield, inflation reduces your future buying power. From the investor's
point of view, eroding value must be offset by an after-tax return high
enough so that real value does not decline.

The problem is in the selection of investments that will not deteriorate
in value, but that also do not contain what are considered excessive risks.
Once you begin to apply these conflicting tests, you discover that you have
only a narrow range of moderately risky investments from which to select.

Example: The most conservative investor may be willing to settle
for very low-yielding products. As a result, on an after-tax basis,
the yield is lower than the rate of inflation. An investment yields
a 4 percent return; however, the rate of inflation is 3 percent and
the investor pays taxes at the rate of 28 percent. An investment of
$100 loses value each year:

Amount Invested	$100.00
Annual Return, 4%	$ 4.00
Less: Income Tax, 28%	− 1.12
After-tax Yield	$ 2.88
After-tax Account Value	$102.88
Less: Inflation, 3%	− 3.09
Net Value after Inflation	$ 99.79

In comparison, the speculator seeks the highest possible returns, to beat inflation on an after-tax basis. But to do so, he also risks substantial losses. For the moderate investor—and that's the majority of individuals—these two extremes must be balanced out. Somewhere in the middle, the moderate investor seeks an acceptable level of risk that, on an after-tax basis, yields a rate of return above the current rate of inflation.

To realistically determine the future inflation rate, you cannot depend strictly on the Consumer Price Index. That index includes increases in the prices of autos and homes each year, representing a significant portion of the total rate. So unless you purchase a new automobile and a new home every year, you will not suffer the published rate of inflation.

If you are purchasing a home that is financed with an adjustable-rate mortgage (ARM), you are probably more susceptible to the published rate of inflation than is the homeowner with a fixed-rate mortgage. But even then, most ARM contracts limit (or *cap*) the amount of increase that can be applied each year; and the contract usually also has a lifetime cap. So for the long term, *your* inflation rate is probably lower than the CPI. As with taxes, we cannot know the future rate of inflation. Consequently, we must apply an *estimate* to our own financial plan, and then use that estimate in evaluating and comparing all of our choices. However, it is a mistake to use the standard retirement formula for estimating future inflation. Under that formula, you are asked to assume an average rate of inflation in order to determine what you will need in retirement.

The problem with that approach is that even the rate you assume won't necessarily apply to you when you do retire. For example, if you will own your home free and clear by retirement date, you will not need to allow for housing expenses. Those expenses might be factors during the years you're paying on a mortgage; but they will not affect your standard of living during retirement.

Salespeople encourage their clients to assume higher rates of inflation than will apply to them realistically. The greater your retirement needs (under an assumed set of predictions), the greater your need for planning today, as the argument goes. Thus, from the salesperson's point of view, the client will have to make decisions today to plan far ahead in order to survive after retirement.

Example: You plan to retire in 25 years, and a financial planner asks you to estimate future inflation and your retirement living expenses. You assume an average rate of 5 percent inflation, and living expenses at $2,000 per month in today's dollars.

One additional assumption you will have to make is the yield you can expect to earn on a savings account and other investments after retirement. If you assume you will earn 10 percent, how much must you save every year to meet your retirement needs?

First, you must calculate the effects of inflation at 5 percent per year. Assuming annual compounding of that rate, the total effect of inflation will be a factor of 3.386355 (factor from the accumulated value of 1 table). That means your monthly living expenses will be:

$$3.386355 \times \$2,000 = \$6,772.71.$$

To calculate the annual income you will need, multiply the inflation-adjusted living expense total by 12:

$$\$6,772.71 \times 12 = \$81,272.52.$$

This calculation states that you will need more than $81,000 per year to survive in retirement. If you can earn 10 percent from your investments, you will need approximately $800,000 in order to afford to retire in 25 years.

The flaw in this calculation is the inflation rate. You must understand that the estimated retirement needs must be assumed to be on an after-tax basis, meaning substantially more must be saved than the $800,000 target amount. But the estimated of *your* inflation rate may be far too high, given that you will own your home and probably will not buy a new automobile every year.

COMPUTING YOUR BREAKEVEN

A more realistic way to plan your future is to make your assumptions on a different premise: that as long as you *match or beat* the rate of inflation, on an after-tax basis, you are not losing money. If you accumulate sufficient assets on that basis, you will have an adequate fund for your retirement —assuming you are putting away funds for that purpose.

How much must you earn today in order to match or surpass the current rate of inflation, as it applies to you? This must be calculated on an after-tax basis, so it is necessary to factor in the rate you pay in federal and state income taxes.

Example: You assume that the average inflation rate is 4 percent. And the combined federal and state tax rate you estimate for this year will be 31 percent. In order to calculate your breakeven, follow these steps:

1. Estimate your after-tax rate of return by deducting your estimated tax rate from 100:

$$100 - 31 = 69.$$

2. Divide 4 (inflation rate) by the answer to step 1.

The result of this calculation, 5.80 percent, is your yield. As long as your investment yields are equal to this, you are matching inflation. And if your yields exceed that rate, your after-tax and after-inflation net worth has grown. The formula for breakeven is shown in Figure 4.2.

Your assumptions concerning your own tax rate and the rate of inflation you will experience should be used to judge any investment you consider. The test must involve two questions:

1. Is this investment likely to beat my after-tax and after-inflation breakeven point?
2. Are the risks acceptable?

If you cannot find investments that yield a rate above your required breakeven point, you should question both the assumptions you've made and your definition of "acceptable" risks. If you are unwilling to take risks beyond the most conservative levels, you may not be able to match or beat the breakeven point. And if you have been too pessimistic regarding inflation, your breakeven will be overstated.

There is a direct relationship between high inflation and high interest rates. Thus, if you assume an inflation rate of only 2 percent, you can build in a great deal of safety at low yields, and still beat the breakeven rate.

$$\frac{I}{100 - T} = B$$

I = inflation rate
T = tax rate
B = breakeven interest rate

FIGURE 4.2   Breakeven.

When inflation is high, you can have a comparable amount of safety with much greater yields.

To compare breakeven yields at various rates of inflation and for various tax rates, refer to the table in Figure 4.3.

Judging the effects of taxes and inflation on your portfolio and future net worth is an uncertain process. You cannot know the future, and can only use the information available to you today. However, to avoid estimating incorrectly, identify and then avoid the flaws that are commonly associated with the process. Do not accept the CPI as the rate of inflation that will necessarily affect your own financial health; and avoid accepting levels of risk you cannot afford, just for the sake of meeting the after-tax rate you desire.

In the next chapter, we will explore the mathematical aspects of fundamental analysis, the study of financial results, and estimates in the investment decision.

TAX BRACKET	INFLATION RATE				
	2%	4%	6%	8%	10%
28%	2.78%	5.56%	8.33%	11.11%	13.89%
29	2.82	5.63	8.45	11.27	14.08
30	2.86	5.71	8.57	11.43	14.29
31	2.90	5.80	8.70	11.59	14.49
32	2.94	5.88	8.82	11.76	14.71
33	2.99	5.97	8.96	11.94	14.93

FIGURE 4.3   Breakeven table.

5

Fundamental Analysis

Stock market investments should be selected in one of two ways: by fundamental or by technical analysis. Fundamental analysis is the study of a company's financial statements—the balance sheet and income statement—and related trends. Technical analysis is based on price movements and pattern trends.

In this chapter, the various methods of evaluating financial strength and trends will be explained. In any form of investment analysis, we must keep in mind that an isolated fact—such as the current level of profits, assets, debts, or sales—is made meaningful only when reviewed in comparison. Accordingly, a review of today's ratios and rates of return is significant only as it relates to historical information of the same nature.

Fundamental analysis should be applied to a company as the last entry in a trend. The longer the period studied, the more dependable the information.

Example: A corporation earned a profit last year of 7 percent of sales (return on sales, as explained in the chapter dealing with rates of return). Is this a positive or a negative result?

The only way you can determine the answer to that question is to compare the return to the same company's return last year, or to a standard. Typically, standards will include data on other corporations in the same industry; a widely understood acceptable result; or a result you develop on your own.

1. **The Same Company's Previous Return:** Depending on the fundamental information you are evaluating, a positive result can be an increase, a decrease, or a stable answer. Sales volume and net worth are expected to increase each year. It is desirable for the rate of costs and expenses to remain consistent or to fall. And net profits should remain at stable, acceptable levels.

69

2. **Other Corporations:**   One widely used method for selecting stock in publicly traded companies is to first select an industry (based on economic trends pointing to favorable conditions), and then to pick the strongest competitor in that industry, based on fundamental signs.

3. **Widely Understood Acceptable Results:**   Some fundamental tests are applied to all companies, with a predetermined level as the acceptable norm. For example, the current ratio (discussed later in this chapter) should be 2 to 1 or better.

4. **Your Own Standard:**   Investors may select stocks based on a combination of risk evaluation factors, such as the dividend rate, price history, level of volatility, and other tests. You may decide in advance to select companies whose stock yields a dividend rate of 7 percent or more, for example.

Fundamental (and technical) analysis can be applied to investments other than stocks. The bond, options, futures, real estate, mutual fund, and other markets all may be analyzed with special tests of their own. The tests appropriate to each of these specialized markets are explained in later chapters.

In the chapter dealing with rates of return, several formulas that define profit and yield were explained. These are fundamental tests. In this chapter, we will describe fundamental formulas in three classifications: earnings ratios, balance sheet ratios, and ratios dealing with profit and value.

EARNINGS RATIOS

One of the best known fundamental tests is also one of the most controversial. The price/earnings ratio is a formula that compares the current market price of stock with the earnings per share.

The formula reveals what multiple of earnings a share of stock sells for; this is used as an indicator of market popularity. As a general rule, the higher the P/E ratio, the greater the expectation of profit from investing in shares. But at the same time, a high P/E also indicates increased risks. The ratio is historical. It compares today's market price with the previous year's earnings per share. Because of this, the P/E ratio is not always a dependable indicator of tomorrow's trend.

The formula changes each time the price of the stock moves upward or downward, and each time a 12-month earning period is reported. Not only is price in the short term likely to change frequently; the earnings as reported may be subject to later revision, or could be distorted due to accounting interpretations. Thus, the P/E ratio, while widely used, is not always accurate, even if analysts could agree on its significance. The opinions among professionals as to the P/E's meaning and value vary widely.

Market price is divided by the reported earnings per share, and the answer is expressed as a single number, representing the multiple of earnings at which the stock is selling. The formula for P/E ratio is shown in Figure 5.1.

Investors who are troubled by the use of earnings to judge a stock's demand or volatility may prefer to use the less commonly known price/sales ratio. This is a formula that compares market price to sales per share of common stock.

Sales are less likely to be distorted or misrepresented through accounting interpretations, or changed by independent audit. Moreover, sales results are often readily available from one period to another, unlike earnings reports, which may be delayed two months or more after the end of a reporting period.

Another advantage of this ratio is that it can be applied even when a company reports a net loss. The P/E ratio cannot be used when a loss is reported, so development of a trend is not always possible.

To compute the price/sales ratio, the current market price is divided by sales per share of common stock. The answer is expressed as a percentage.

Investors who use any ratio involving current market price must recognize the market factors involved. Price is not a strict fundamental, as are the assets, liabilities, and net worth reported on the balance sheet, or the sales, costs, expenses, and profits reported on the income statement.

Price reflects the broad perception of value for shares of stock, with all of the known fundamental and technical information taken into account. The price is discounted for negative reports, and increases in response to

$$\frac{MP}{EPS} = PE$$

MP = market price
EPS = earnings per share
PE = price/earnings ratio

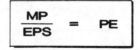

$$\frac{22}{1.08} = 20.4$$

FIGURE 5.1   Price/earnings ratio.

good news (such as higher than expected earnings). However, the current price does not always reflect true value of stock in the long run. It does reflect demand at the moment. Realizing this flaw in the use of price in any analysis, a true fundamentalist will concentrate only on financial results, and will equate the price to those results in the search for buying opportunities, or to time a sale.

The most widely reported and used pure fundamental test is earnings per share of common stock. The *primary* earnings per share does not account for potential earnings in the event that convertible bonds and preferred stock are converted, and is the most commonly used form of the ratio. Rather, it reports the earnings per share based on the current number of shares of common stock outstanding.

To compute earnings per share, divide net earnings by the number of shares of common stock outstanding. Net earnings is the amount of net income, less dividends paid to preferred stockholders. The formula for primary earnings per share is shown in Figure 5.2.

A second form of this calculation is called *fully diluted earnings per share*. This calculates earnings potential if convertible bonds and preferred stock are converted. Convertible bonds and preferred stock may be exchanged for a specified number of shares in common stock. The fully diluted calculation estimates earnings per share in the event of conversion. To calculate, divide the sum of net earnings plus the conversion value, by the number of outstanding shares of common stock after conversion.

"Conversion value" refers to the change that would occur in net earnings in the event of conversion. For example, interest is paid on outstanding bonds. However, if those bonds are converted, the interest will not be

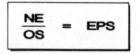

$$\frac{NE}{OS} = EPS$$

NE = net earnings (net income less preferred dividends)

OS = outstanding shares of common stock

EPS = earnings per share

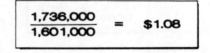

$$\frac{1,736,000}{1,601,000} = \$1.08$$

FIGURE 5.2   Primary earnings per share.

paid. The liability is replaced when bonds are exchanged for common stock. Thus, the amount of interest is the conversion value of a convertible bond.

In the event of conversion, the number of outstanding shares of common stock would be increased. To correctly report fully diluted earnings per share, both the conversion-based income and the number of common shares must be recalculated. The formula for fully diluted earnings per share is shown in Figure 5.3.

Another earnings ratio compares dividends paid on common stock to net income. Dividends are usually evaluated on the basis of yield: a comparison of the dividend paid per share, and the share price. However, that yield is in a constant state of change, because market price is not a stable factor; neither is it purely a fundamental number. Thus, an investor might look unfavorably on a stock today because the yield is lower than an assumed standard. However, the same stock could fall into an acceptable range next week—without any change in the dividend payment—because the stock's price has dropped.

Example: Last month, a stock was selling for $35 per share, and the dividend is $1.65 per share. The dividend yield is 4.7 percent. You have established a personal standard that a stock you purchase must yield 5 percent or more. This month, the stock's price has fallen to $29, and the dividend is still $1.65 per share. The yield now is 5.7 percent.

The dividend is the same, and the stock's market price has fallen —perhaps an indication that the company is experiencing financial

$$\frac{NE + CV}{OSC} = FD$$

NE = net earnings
CV = conversion value
OSC = outstanding shares after conversion
FD = fully diluted earnings per share

$$\frac{1,736,000 + 600,000}{2,301,000} = \$1.02$$

FIGURE 5.3 Fully diluted earnings per share.

problems, and has fallen out of favor. The reduced price reflects lower demand. However, on the basis of dividend yield alone, the stock now meets your criteria.

The obvious flaw in evaluating stocks based solely on dividend yield is corrected by applying a different fundamental test, which does not involve the ever-changing market price factor. The payout ratio compares dividends on common stock to net income (adjusted for dividends paid on preferred stock), and the result is expressed as a percentage. This ratio will report a true increase in dividend yield, and is more dependable when followed as part of a trend. It employs strictly fundamental information, and thus is not distorted by ever-changing market factors, as reflected in the current price. The formula for payout ratio is shown in Figure 5.4.

BALANCE SHEET RATIOS

The second series of ratios is used to analyze financial strength of a company, represented by what is reported on the balance sheet. Investors are concerned with two major factors here: the consistent and well-managed level and strength of working capital, and the relative status of capitalization.

Working capital is the difference between current assets (cash and assets convertible to cash within one year) and current liabilities (debts payable within one year). Every company must manage its working capital, so that the day-to-day and month-to-month operating costs and expenses can be funded from cash flow. Without adequate working capital, a company must depend heavily on borrowings; this requirement translates to excessive interest expense.

$$\frac{CD}{NI - PD} = PR$$

CD = dividends on common stock
NI = net income
PD = dividends on preferred stock
PR = payout ratio

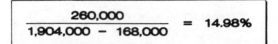

$$\frac{260,000}{1,904,000 - 168,000} = 14.98\%$$

FIGURE 5.4   Payout ratio.

Capitalization takes two forms: debt and equity. An "acceptable" level of debt varies from one situation to another. But as a general rule, investors must be concerned with the relative degree of debt capitalization, when compared to the trend in equity (common and preferred stock). When the organization can increase its earnings at a rate greater than the cost of borrowing money, debt is a positive factor. However, when the company is forced to borrow to continue operations or to make up for lacking cash flow, interest drains profits.

The best-known balance sheet test is the current ratio. Current assets are divided by current liabilities, and the answer is expressed as "x" to 1. A current ratio of 2 to 1 or better is considered acceptable. When the ratio falls below that level, it is an indication that working capital is not being well planned or managed. The exception to this is the case where the sheer volume of cash is so great that the ratio cannot be applied. In many of the largest corporations that trade publicly, ample cash is available to fund operations, so that the 2-to-1 test becomes insignificant. The formula for the current ratio is shown in Figure 5.5.

Because current assets include inventory, the current ratio cannot be applied in companies where the inventory is not a significant factor in the analysis of working capital. For example, for a corporation that maintains inventory but makes most of its sales by providing a service, the current ratio is not very revealing. In these cases, the quick-assets ratio (also called the acid test or liquidity ratio) should be used.

Even in those organizations where inventory is directly related to the generation of income, the quick-assets ratio can provide useful fundamental information. As is true with all ratios, an analysis should be performed not in isolation, but as part of a trend. A generally acceptable quick-assets ratio is 1 to 1 or better.

$$\frac{CA}{CL} = CR$$

CA = current assets
CL = current liabilities
CR = current ratio

$$\frac{8,915,432}{4,101,926} = 2.17 \text{ to } 1$$

FIGURE 5.5 Current ratio.

The quick-assets ratio is calculated by dividing current assets minus inventory, by current liabilities. The formula for this ratio is shown in Figure 5.6.

Another ratio concerned with cash flow is working capital turnover. This is a comparison between gross sales for a specified period (one year in most cases) and the working capital amount (current assets minus current liabilities). One problem with this ratio is that sales extend over a period of time, while working capital exists at a single moment. Whether a comparison between these two financial numbers is relevant is a question that must always be asked. Since working capital can change drastically during the sales period, the ratio does not always reflect a true picture. Analyzing this ratio as part of a trend may help rectify the problem; however, seasonal changes may hide a widely fluctuating turnover result.

The formula for working capital turnover is shown in Figure 5.7.

A second group of balance sheet ratios is concerned with comparisons of debt and equity. The first test in this group is the debt/equity ratio, a comparison of liabilities to tangible net worth.

Tangible net worth is the sum of shareholders' equity, minus intangible assets (such as goodwill, covenants not to compete, and other assets lacking physical value). The formula is expressed as a percentage, and reports the portion of debt representing total capitalization. As part of a trend, a rising debt/equity ratio is a negative indicator. It shows that the corporation is funding operations through debt on an increasing basis. The formula for debt/equity ratio is shown in Figure 5.8.

Total capitalization is divided into three broad groups:

1. Bonds (long-term debt).
2. Preferred stock.

$$\frac{CA - I}{CL} = QA$$

CA = current assets
I = inventory
CL = current liabilities
QA = quick assets ratio

$$\frac{8,915,432 - 4,000,000}{4,101,926} = 1.20 \text{ to } 1$$

FIGURE 5.6   Quick-assets ratio.

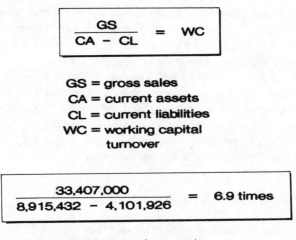

$$\frac{GS}{CA - CL} = WC$$

GS = gross sales
CA = current assets
CL = current liabilities
WC = working capital
turnover

$$\frac{33,407,000}{8,915,432 - 4,101,926} = 6.9 \text{ times}$$

FIGURE 5.7 Working capital turnover.

3. Common stock plus capital surplus plus retained earnings (share-holder's equity).

A series of ratios reports the portion of total capitalization that each of these groups represents. Over a period of time, trends reporting increases or decreases in the relative size of each group will indicate whether management is attempting to retire its debts, maintain a capitalization relationship, or depend more heavily on borrowings to fund operations. For the long-term investor, an ever-increasing equity percentage indicates increased net worth. However, debt capitalization is worthwhile as long as the profits from the use of funds exceed interest costs.

The first of three tests is called the bond ratio. This is derived by

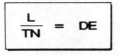

$$\frac{L}{TN} = DE$$

L = total liabilities
TN = tangible net worth
DE = debt/equity ratio

$$\frac{12,101,926}{14,754,000} = 82.02\%$$

FIGURE 5.8 Debt/equity ratio.

dividing the bond liability by total capitalization (bonds, preferred stock, and common shareholders' equity). The formula is shown in Figure 5.9.

The second test measures the preferred stock portion of total capitalization. The formula is summarized in Figure 5.10.

The third test is the common stock ratio, which involves the combined values of common stock, capital surplus, and retained earnings—collectively referred to as common shareholders' equity. The sum of these is divided by total capitalization, as shown in Figure 5.11.

The addition of percentages for the bond, preferred stock, and common stock ratios is 100 percent of total capitalization.

PROFIT AND VALUE RATIOS

The third group of fundamental tests is concerned with ratios involving income in relation to interest and dividend expenses; operating expenses; the margin of profit; and book value per share.

The first test, interest coverage, reports the degree to which a corporation provides for the payment of interest on its bonds. The result is shown in the "number of times," or multiples that earnings exceed the interest paid or owed. As a general rule, a multiple of 4 or more is considered a healthy level of interest coverage.

The amount of earnings before interest and taxes is divided by the interest expense on bonds, as reported in Figure 5.12.

Preferred dividend coverage reports a similar status, but rather than involving interest, this test compares net income to dividends paid to preferred stockholders. The formula is shown in Figure 5.13.

The expense ratio (also called operating ratio) is a calculation that reports the total of costs and expenses, compared to net sales. Included in

$$\frac{B}{TC} = R$$

B = bonds
TC = total capitalization
R = bond ratio

$$\frac{8,000,000}{24,855,000} = 32.19\%$$

FIGURE 5.9   Bond ratio.

$$\frac{P}{TC} = R$$

P = preferred stock
TC = total capitalization
R = preferred stock ratio

$$\frac{2,101,000}{24,855,000} = 8.45\%$$

FIGURE 5.10   Preferred stock ratio.

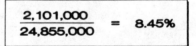

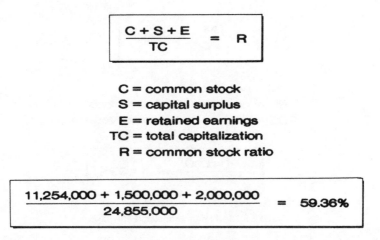

$$\frac{C + S + E}{TC} = R$$

C = common stock
S = capital surplus
E = retained earnings
TC = total capitalization
R = common stock ratio

$$\frac{11,254,000 + 1,500,000 + 2,000,000}{24,855,000} = 59.36\%$$

FIGURE 5.11 Common stock ratio.

costs and expenses is the amount of depreciation claimed on fixed assets. Net sales represents the gross sales reported, minus returns and allowances. This calculation is the opposite of margin of profit (also called return on sales).

The formula for expense ratio is shown in Figure 5.14.

Margin of profit is calculated by dividing operating income by net sales. Operating income is the amount remaining on the income statement after deducting costs, expenses and depreciation. The formula for margin of profit is shown in Figure 5.15.

Our final calculation is for book value per share of common stock. There is almost always a difference between book value per share and market value, in some cases a substantial difference. In many industries,

$$\frac{E}{I} = IC$$

E = earnings before interest and taxes
I = bond interest
IC = interest coverage

$$\frac{3,053,000}{600,000} = 5.09 \text{ times}$$

FIGURE 5.12 Interest coverage.

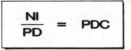

$$\frac{NI}{PD} = PDC$$

NI = net income
PD = preferred stock dividends
PDC = preferred dividend coverage

$$\frac{1,904,000}{168,000} = 11.33\%$$

FIGURE 5.13   Preferred dividend coverage.

in-demand shares sell for multiples above book value, while out-of-favor or very stable stocks may hold a market price well below book value (these are referred to as discounted stocks).

Book value is the tangible, actual value of a share of stock, ignoring changes due to market demand or perceived value. It is calculated by adding common stock, capital surplus, and retained earnings (collectively, shareholders' equity), and then subtracting any intangible assets. The net of that calculation is then divided by the number of outstanding shares of common stock. The value is expressed as a dollar amount, as shown in Figure 5.16.

$$\frac{CG + OE + D}{NS} = ER$$

CG = cost of goods sold
OE = operating expenses
D = depreciation
NS = net sales
ER = expense ratio

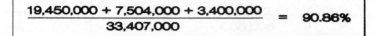

$$\frac{19,450,000 + 7,504,000 + 3,400,000}{33,407,000} = 90.86\%$$

FIGURE 5.14   Expense ratio.

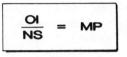

$$\frac{OI}{NS} = MP$$

OI = operating income
NS = net sales
MP = margin of profit

$$\frac{3,053,000}{33,407,000} = 9.14\%$$

FIGURE 5.15   Margin of profit.

Other Fundamental Trends

Fundamental analysis is not restricted to the calculation of ratios. It may include any study of financial information reported by a corporation; or of news that will affect the fundamentals.

Example: Tracking the trend in gross sales is a fundamental test. A company's growth may be judged by a study of gross sales over a period of years.

$$\frac{C + S + E - I}{OS} = BV$$

C = common stock
S = capital surplus
E = retained earnings
I = intangible assets
OS = number of outstanding shares
BV = book value per share

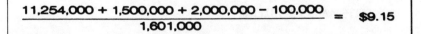

$$\frac{11,254,000 + 1,500,000 + 2,000,000 - 100,000}{1,601,000} = \$9.15$$

FIGURE 5.16   Book value per share.

Analysis of news concerning a company's financial strength, management, or competitive position is fundamental, since these factors are expected to affect profits and equity.

Example: If a drug company develops a revolutionary new drug, the news of that drug's approval for sale is expected to increase the company's profits and its competitive position.

Example: A corporation announces the appointment of a new CEO. The change may be perceived as a positive change if the market expects improved fundamentals as a result.

Example: Two corporations merge, forming a larger and better financed entity. This eliminates competition and improves the fundamentals of both former groups. The news of acquisitions, takeovers, and mergers is an important fundamental test. Rumors of pending takeovers certainly play an important role in buying and selling decisions in the market.

Example: Although a company's fundamental position is strong, the industry as a whole is out of favor. As a result, the fundamentals of the industry may overrule the favorable situation of one corporation. This may be reflected in a declining market price, even when the fundamental strength of the company is not changed. A corporation primarily associated with one industry may earn the majority of its profits from other activities; even so, the industry fundamentals could prove more significant in terms of investment value.

A distinction must be made between fundamental value and investment value. The fundamentals may be highly favorable, but the investment is not—in terms of timing. A company may be selling far below its book values, earning a profit above expectations, and meeting all of the fundamental tests you apply. And yet investment value is poor because, at this time, the company or the industry is not looked upon favorably. Investment value is not always rooted in the fundamentals, and the pure accounting logic of fundamental analysis often fades in significance. When market sentiment is negative, the demand for shares of a company will fall, and the market price follows—regardless of fundamental strength.

BENEFITS AND PROBLEMS

Without fundamental analysis, investors would have no dependable basis for evaluating a company's ability to remain in business. When a large number of companies are compared for fundamental strength, the leaders become obvious. Their sales are consistent or growing; profits and dividend yield are higher than those of less established competitors; and capitalization is properly managed, with ratios maintained at acceptable levels.

Investors use fundamental analysis in many forms, usually not relying on only one indicator to make decisions about buying, holding, or selling stock. They may also combine fundamental and technical information.

An intrinsic problem with the fundamentals is that we are always looking *backwards*. Fundamentals can be used to predict the future, but predictions cannot anticipate drastic changes in investment value. And we must always assume that the current market price of a security already reflects the publicly known fundamental information. If that is the case, then fundamentals are of little real value in selecting investments.

The fundamentals may not tell the story of a company's future and, even combined with technical analysis, do not always tell the whole story. Most companies cannot be judged purely by analysis of any kind. The trends that fundamental analysis reveal do not always mean the same thing in two different companies.

Example: You are considering buying the stock of a publicly traded corporation. In checking various fundamental indicators, you discover that gross sales fell during the two latest years. What does this mean?

Falling sales are almost always a negative sign. This could signify that:

- The company is losing sales to a stronger competitor.
- Poor customer service or product quality is threatening the company's strength.
- Mismanagement is the cause of the problem.
- Labor difficulties are preventing the company from maintaining its sales record.

The trend might be due to any of these negative factors. You can discover the truth only with a more in-depth analysis, using a brokerage firm's research department or an independent research and analysis service (such as Value Line or Standard & Poor's).

The trend could even be a *positive* one. This can be revealed only by looking beyond the seemingly obvious results. For example, the company may have increased its sales for several years, only to report lower net profits and a reduction in quality. Management may have responded by eliminating unprofitable outlets, favoring greater profits, better product quality, customer service, and a positive corporate reputation, over ever-growing gross sales.

The fundamentals should be thought of as valuable tools in your decision-making process. However, you must also realize that the pure mathematical evaluation of a company does not tell the whole story.

The next chapter explains how technical analysis is used by investors. Unlike the financial information that forms the basis for the fundamentals, technical analysis deals only with price and volume trends.

6

Technical Analysis

While the fundamental analyst depends on financial information as the means for determining worthwhile investment decisions, the technician is more concerned with trends. A technician believes that market movements occur in predictable patterns, and that profitable decisions must be made by recognizing the direction those trends dictate—often by taking action opposite to the prevailing sentiment.

Technicians, for the most part, are contrarian investors. They believe that the majority of investors are wrong most of the time, including professional money managers. Some market realities bear out this belief.

Example: Historical buying and selling patterns do indicate that the market, as a whole, overreacts to market news and times decisions poorly. As the market trend reaches a high—and immediately before it reverses—buying is usually at a peak as well. And when the market reaches the bottom, selling activity will have accelerated.

Example: Market highs may be signalled by record numbers of new investors coming into the market as buyers (this certainly occurred immediately before the crash of 1987). It may also be signalled by a peak in issues reaching 52-week high prices.

The contrarian theory holds validity, in the recognition that the majority cannot be right all of the time. But investors must also recognize that there are no secret formulas for guaranteed success. Only half of all the stocks will perform above the average. The other half must perform below average. This is not a theory—it is *mathematical fact.* In order for a given number of winners to exist, there must be an equal number of losers. This is the definition of "average," and this reality often is overlooked by market analysts.

In this chapter, many of the popular technical indicators will be explained and placed in context. We will examine the popular technical theories and the use of market indexes, and then describe indicators as they apply to price movement, volume, and volatility.

THE TECHNICAL DILEMMA

As an investor, you must decide which forms of available information to use. Your dilemma, though, is that a mountain of information is available. Determining which is valid and which is not is itself a formidable task.

This problem has been compounded in recent years with the application of technical analysis in automated systems. With widespread use of home computers, it is now possible to apply the most complex technical indicators with very little effort. The problem in this available technology is that users do not always understand the premise of the mathematical study.

Is the technical test a valid one? That is the question that every investor must face. Virtually every form of variable in the market has been measured by someone, and formed into a technical theory—even using data far beyond the market itself. The danger in this is that investors may become convinced that secret formulas—even mystical secrets for successful investing—do, indeed, exist. And that is simply not true.

The existence of a certain way to market profits would, as a mathematical inevitability, defeat itself. The law of averages dictates that potential profit is limited by the degree of potential loss. If everyone had a formula for certain success, that very factor would undo itself. Our auction market depends on perceptions of investors to dictate its path. Supply and demand are matched and transactions are executed. But even with this absolute logic firmly in mind, many investors continually search for magic formulas, following one guru or another to promised secrets of wealth.

It seems that, with the vast number of technical indicators in use, the rule is: If it moves, measure it. The approach often is a backward one. First, historical information is collected and interpreted in search of some revealing trend. That information may be distorted to self-fulfill the analyst's desire for results. Or certain information is ignored during one period and pointedly highlighted during another. Then, when a trend is discovered, it becomes the basis for predicting the future.

With enough of the right kind of interpretation, any information can be made to appear dependable. However, as many investors have discovered, a look forward is much more difficult than a look backward. Thus, technical analysis must be approached with caution. Depending too heavily on a single indicator, theory, or market factor will not produce the desired results.

Keeping in mind that, on average, only half of all stocks will perform above the average, technical analysis must serve as one of many tools in the investor's hands. Do not make the mistake of believing that the formula for investing success can be determined by purchasing a computer program, reading a newsletter, or applying a simple rule. Investing success must be the result of diligent research, intelligent analysis, and a degree of timing and luck.

Technical analysis is best used in recognition of the fact that the market reacts not to singular influences, nor to predetermined trends. Certain technical information, when used in combination with other sources of knowledge, will be helpful to you in making informed and timely decisions. But you cannot expect to create consistent and dependable profits by using past information alone.

TECHNICAL THEORIES

Two important theories operate in the market, and are in conflict with one another. These are the Random Walk Hypothesis and the Dow Theory.

The Random Walk Hypothesis is based on the writings of Louis Bachelier, who in 1900 published a paper called "Theory of Speculation." The theory states that all forms of technical and fundamental analysis are of no use or validity. Rather, prices move in an entirely random manner. The hypothesis claims that no study of the past can reveal future price movement.

Trends, the hypothesis states, cannot be tracked because they are completely random. In fact, the data that an analyst selects creates a trend. Most technicians disagree, claiming that trends in data point to future price movement in a dependable manner.

Proponents of the Random Walk Hypothesis believe that, if the market is efficient, then the current prices of all securities reflect all known information, both fundamental and technical. In an efficient market, all stocks are fairly priced, based on the perception of value in the market as a whole. Thus, selection itself becomes random because all securities have an equal likelihood of moving upward or downward in the future.

The second theory dominates the field of technical analysis. The Dow Theory is based on the editorials published by Charles H. Dow in the *Wall Street Journal* between 1900 and 1902. Dow created the well-known Dow Jones Industrial Averages (DJIA) and a second index, the Dow Jones Rail Averages (today called Transportation Averages). A third average, Utilities, has been added, to expand on the thoughts expressed by Charles Dow.

The basic principle stated by the Dow Theory is that the future direction of prices is recognizable and predictable, based on market signals. It defines three forms of price movement:

1. **Primary Movement:**   Also called a major trend, the primary movement extends for one year or more, and establishes an upward
   movement (bull market) or a downward movement (bear market).

2. **Secondary Reaction:**   This is also called an intermediate reaction
   or trend. It lasts from a few weeks to several months, and is characterized by price movements in a direction opposite that of the
   primary movement.

3. **Minor Trend:**   This includes daily fluctuations in price movement,
   and may last from a few hours or days to several weeks.

The Dow Theory recognizes that all changes in price, volume, company
news, and other factors, as constantly updated, affect overall perceptions
in the market, both today and in the future. Judgments about the trend
and the duration of price movements are constantly being adjusted as new
information comes to light.

The significance of new information, according to the Dow Theory, is
determined by confirming signals. For example, when one index establishes a major shift in the trend, it must be confirmed by a corresponding
change in one of the other Dow Jones indexes. In addition to a confirmation,
the trend must hold for a period of time in order to qualify as a signal of
change.

The Dow Theory is very difficult to use in a practical, everyday application. This is so because it does not claim to identify the duration of a
trend. There is no long-term predictability in the Dow Theory, since the
actual performance of the market depends on many factors outside of the
market: government regulation, health of the economy, and political actions and conditions.

Some technicians have attempted to reduce market analysis to a purely
mathematical science. The Elliott Wave Principle, named for R.N. Elliott,
who published a series of articles in *Financial World* in 1939, is one such
approach.

Elliott identified a mathematical rhythm in the market, based on the
theory that all things in nature move and react in rhythmic cycles. The
pattern of those cycles, Elliott claimed, is predictable.

The theory is based on application of the Fibonacci Sequence, a phe-
nomenon described by a 13th century mathematician named Leonardo
Fibonacci. This sequence involves an indefinite grouping of integers, in
which each number is equal to the sum of the preceding two numbers.
Elliott claimed that the certainty of mathematical relationships as seen in
nature can also be applied to the changes in value in the market.

The sequence of numbers in the sequence is:

$$1 + 2 = 3$$
$$2 + 3 = 5$$
$$3 + 5 = 8$$
$$5 + 8 = 13$$
$$8 + 13 = 21$$
$$13 + 21 = 34$$
$$- \quad -$$
$$- \quad -$$
$$- \quad -$$

This progressive relationship between the numbers is called a golden section (also called golden triangle) in mathematics. In the Fibonacci Sequence, each number is the sum of the preceding two numbers. In addition, the ratio of each number to the next approximates 0.618 to 1, and the ratio of each number to the preceding approximates 1.618 to 1.

Elliott applied this mathematical pattern to the market, and identified repeating 80-year waves, or trends. The major wave is called the Grand Supercycle, and consists of five waves of increasing prices, and three waves of deceasing prices (3 + 5 = 8 in the Fibonacci Sequence).

The Elliott Wave Principle is an intriguing historical study. However, it must also be pointed out that there may be lapses between one cycle wave and another, or waves within the 80-year period may overlap. Looking back, it is easy to spot the wave periods. However, the imperfections of interpretation bring the theory into question, both as a force of nature and as a practical investment analysis tool.

The successful investor must depend on the timing of each decision. And in that regard, the Elliott Wave Principle is of no practical value. Anticipating intermediate price changes is impossible, and the *direction* of price change cannot be known in advance by applying the Elliott Wave Principle—a factor that cannot be ignored even by the most devoted market mathematician.

The timing of decisions makes a tremendous difference, and the long-term mathematical trends described by Elliott do not allow for this. For example, consider the difference in timing if you had invested money in the stock market at its 1987 peak on August 25, when the Dow Jones Industrial Averages were 2722.42, or after October 19, when the averages were at 1738.74. Obviously, the degree of profit or loss would vary greatly based on the timing decision. In this extreme example, that involves a period of less than two months.

Market Indexes

Market movement is defined in the context of one or more indexes. Indexes are constructed using selective or comprehensive stock data. The best-known of these indexes is the Dow Jones Industrials, which consists of 30 industrial stocks.

It may be assumed that using only 30 issues on only one exchange (the New York Stock Exchange) for an index is a misrepresentation, especially in a market that involves several thousand stocks and a number of regional exchanges. And in fact, there are many days when the market is mixed. For example, the DJIA—also called the "blue chips"—will be up for the day, but the average price per share on the New York Exchange is down. However, the DJIA has gained legitimacy as a market indicator, and has become the barometer of market sentiment. In many respects, the blue chips do lead the market. Many issues rise or fall directly in response to action among the 30 industrials of the DJIA.

The 30 issues in this average represent about 30 percent of the total New York Stock Exchange capitalization, and have consistently represented market movements. To keep the relative composition of the DJIA at the correct level, each of the 30 issues' stock price is adjusted by a divisor. This is necessary due to stock splits, stock dividends, and replacement of one company with another on the DJIA itself. One flaw in this method results when one stock's market price grows without the stock being split. That issue's weight will be greater than the weight of a comparable issue that did split.

The Dow Jones Transportation Averages (20 transportation stocks) and the Dow Jones Utility Averages (15 utilities) are the two additional Dow Jones Averages. The three together are called the Composite Average of the market.

A second index that is widely followed and is broader-based is the Standard & Poor's 500 Index. This index was created in 1957, and includes 400 industrial, 20 transportation, 40 financial, and 40 utility stocks. This index accounts for price movement in about 90 percent of the New York Stock Exchange market value. The price of each share is multiplied by the number of outstanding shares for the company, and that total is then restated as an index value.

The New York Exchange Index is a measure of all listed stocks, and is expressed in dollars and cents rather than in points, as is the DJIA. It was originally set at a value of $50.00, the approximate value of each listed share of stock on December 31, 1965.

The Wilshire 5000 Equity Index reports the value-weighted total of all common stocks traded in the U.S. The index, expressed in billions of dollars of market value, is the most accurate indicator of the market as a whole.

Other indexes of market value are used for measurement of various exchanges, or for selected groupings of stocks by industry. Most investors know that each day's change in an index's value will not necessarily affect the value of holdings. Movements tend to occur in an offsetting manner, so that timing must be accompanied by patience. For example, on Monday the market jumps 35 points (according to the DJIA). This means only that the 30 industrials appreciated by a collective price increase, and not that other issues are affected in the same direction. On Tuesday, the market falls 15 points, again not necessarily meaning that your portfolio is affected by the change. However, stocks not in one particular average might rise and fall according to the trend established by even the most selective of indexes.

Thus, the DJIA, for example, *does* affect the market. However, its proponents claim that it reflects overall market sentiment when, in fact, the market might follow the trend set in the averages—not as part of the overall trend, but in response to the performance among the blue chips.

Another technical index follows trends in three economic indicators—the prime rate, inflation rate, and unemployment rate. This is called the Misery Index.

The collective trend in these three indicators works contrary to the movement of the market, as a rule. When the Misery Index peaks, the market is likely to be at a low (as measured by the DJIA, for example). And when the Misery Index is low, market sentiment is more optimistic. The trend in this index does not anticipate nor predict market movement. Thus, it is not truly a tool for analysis as much as it is a report of current sentiment. It summarizes the way in which investors are affected by economic trends at any specific time.

PRICE MOVEMENT

Technicians are concerned primarily with predicting price movement. This is achieved by following trends in a number of indicators, many based on the Dow Theory and in recognition of primary and secondary movements.

Advancing and Declining Issues

The trends occurring in the relative number of advancing and declining issues are given a great deal of weight in technical analysis. Under the Random Walk Theory, the degree to which advances and declines affect the value or timing of investments is not a factor. But under the Dow Theory, these trends are significant. And in reality, as the market establishes a strong bullish or bearish mood, many issues will follow the trend. Thus, investors can recognize and time their decisions based on one of the many advance/decline tests.

The first test is the advance/decline noncumulative trend, also called the Hughes Breadth Index. Each day's declining issues are subtracted from advancing issues, and the net difference is divided by total issues traded. If declining issues outnumber advancing issues, the result—called the breadth of the market—will be negative. Issues that are unchanged are not counted in the top part of the equation, but are included in the total.

Example: During a week, the market advances and declines are reported as shown in the following table.

	FRI	THU	WED	TUE	MON
Issues Traded	1982	1961	1943	1966	1994
Advances	914	828	901	682	814
Declines	916	1024	956	1203	1106
Unchanged	152	109	86	81	74

The breadth-of-the-market index is computed for Wednesday of this week by subtracting declining issues (956) from advancing issues (901), and dividing the net by the total issues traded (1943). In this case, the percentage breadth will be negative, since declining issues are higher than advancing issues. This calculation is shown in Figure 6.1.

A variation on the breadth of the market is the Absolute Breadth Index, developed by Norman Fosback of the Institute for Econometric Research. This involves subtracting declining issues from advancing ones. The calculation is summarized in Figure 6.2.

The study can also be reduced to a trend in advancing issues alone, or in declining issues alone. This is often done on a moving average basis.

$$\frac{A - D}{T} = B$$

A = advancing issues
D = declining issues
T = total issues
B = breadth of the market

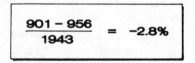

$$\frac{901 - 956}{1943} = -2.8\%$$

FIGURE 6.1   Breadth-of-the-market index.

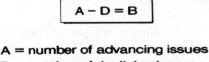

A = number of advancing issues
D = number of declining issues
B = absolute breadth

FIGURE 6.2   Absolute breadth index.

Thus, each day's factor is added to the average factor for a longer period of time, and the oldest day's factor is dropped off.

Example: A seven-week moving average will involve 35 market days. Each calculation of the moving average calls for the addition of the latest day's trend, and the deletion of the oldest day's trend.

The isolated advancing or declining issue trend involves dividing the number by the total number of issues traded, with the result expressed as a percentage. So when advancing issues are 901, and total issues are 1943, it may be said that 46.4 percent of all issues advanced on that day. The formula for advancing and declining issue trends are shown in Figure 6.3.

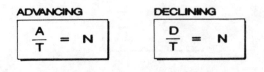

A = number of issues advancing in price
D = number of issues declining in price
T = total issues traded
N = trend

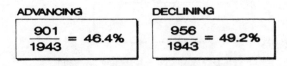

FIGURE 6.3   Advancing and declining issues.

HIGH AND LOW PRICE LEVELS

Besides advancing- and declining-issue studies, the number of issues attaining new high and new low price levels is also studied to determine technical trends. A new high or new low is defined as a price exceeding previous price ranges during the past 52-week period. The trends are usually calculated on a moving average basis.

The new high/new low ratio involves dividing the number of new-high issues by the number of new-low issues. The resulting factor, when studied within the context of a trend, reveals a particular sentiment. As the ratio of new highs grows, the contrarian believes it signals the approach of a market high; and as it becomes a negative (or, when new lows exceed new highs), the sign is that the market is approaching a low. The calculation of the new high/new low ratio is shown in Figure 6.4.

Variations on high and low prices, based on a 52-week period, include:

1. **New Highs:** New highs are tracked on a moving average, representing the number of issues attaining prices higher than their price ranges during the preceding 52 weeks.

2. **New Lows:** New lows are tracked on a moving average, representing the number of issues attaining prices lower than their price ranges during the preceding 52 weeks.

3. **New High - New Low:** The difference between new highs and new lows is tracked on a moving average, representing the number of issues moving above or below their price ranges during the preceding 52 weeks.

$$\frac{NH}{NL} = R$$

NH = number of issues with
new high prices

NL = number of issues with
new low prices

R = new high/new low ratio

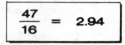
$$\frac{47}{16} = 2.94$$

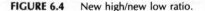

FIGURE 6.4   New high/new low ratio.

CONFIDENCE THEORY

The Confidence Theory is based on the premise that overall investor sentiment dictates price direction. So, as investors become pessimistic, the market may be expected to fall. This can be measured in a variety of ways; the most widely used is Barron's Confidence Index. This employs the study of yields on bonds, as a means for judging stock market confidence. When yields on lower-grade bonds fall, that signals a speculative sentiment in the stock market, and increases in higher-yielding bonds is a sign of growing stock market confidence. The study of bonds, assumes that investor sentiment mandates whether money should be invested in fixed-income securities or in stocks, and to what degree.

Insider Trading

Technicians also follow trends among inside traders, including major stockholders and corporate officers. It is assumed that these individuals are in the best possible position to know when a company's stock is worth holding. Changes in insider buying or selling activity are considered important technical and timing indicators.

Mutual Fund Indicators

Institutional investors—especially mutual funds—account for a majority of the trading activity in the market. Thus, technicians recognize that certain trends in institutional activity will have significant impact on future price movement.

One of the most important of these indicators concerns the amount of cash that mutual funds have on hand. When the cash level is high, it represents pending demand for securities. The theory, then, is that when mutual funds begin to invest their available cash, prices will be driven up by the demand. However, when mutual funds have low reserves of cash on hand, they are near fully invested levels. The contrarian sees this as a signal that prices will fall in the near future.

The mutual fund cash-to-assets ratio involves dividing cash and cash equivalents by the total assets of the fund. The resulting percentage is the cash availability for mutual funds. The ratio is shown in Figure 6.5.

A high ratio of cash is a bullish signal, as it reflects professional management sentiment that is believed to be wrong. The contrarian believes that fund management is usually wrong at market extremes—cautious when the market is at a low, and overly optimistic when it is at a high. So buying power of the institutional investor is used as a means for deciding when to buy or sell stocks.

C = cash and cash equivalents
A = total fund assets
R = cash to assets ratio

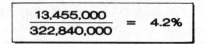

FIGURE 6.5   Cash-to-assets ratio.

Earnings-Per-Share Ranking

Any discussion of the technical analysis of prices cannot be complete without mentioning earnings per share. While this, by itself, is considered a fundamental indicator, overall trends and changes in EPS are often used for technical purposes.

One application is seen in the Earnings-Per-Share Ranking as published by *Investors Daily* for listed stocks. Each issue is ranked from 0 to 99, based on growth in EPS during the last five years. A ranking of 80 or better is considered superior, representing the top 20 percent of all issues.

Some investors may select stocks based on a superior rating alone. However, like any technical or trend indicator, this could prove a dangerous practice. Remember that a ranking based on historical information is a look backward. Hindsight will *not* always indicate the future. A worthwhile application of this information is to seek issues with a consistent record of superior ranking over the long term. And that information, combined with other technical and fundamental tests, may be used to define your investing standards.

VOLUME INDICATORS

In addition to tracking price by a number of market indicators, technicians pay attention to trends in volume—for individual stocks, for industry groups, or for the market as a whole.

Any large percentage change, or change in the number of shares traded during a day, week, or longer period may represent a significant trend to the technician. The manner in which this information is interpreted depends on the other technical indicators employed.

Block Trading

A large block is defined as a single trade of 10,000 shares or more. Institutional investors trade in large blocks, so institutional trends are tracked by following large-block volume. Since institutions represent the largest portion of dollar and share volume in the market, institutional trends are important.

The large-block ratio is calculated by dividing the volume in large-block trading, by the total volume for the same period (day, week, month, etc.). The resulting percentage is the portion of the market represented by block trading. This calculation is shown in Figure 6.6.

New Issues

Many technicians follow the trends in new issues on the market, tracking the rate at which they appear, investor response, or performance during the first few months the shares are available. Each of these trends is used to judge market sentiment, and then to anticipate future price movement.

Contrarians recognize that, as markets reach bullish peaks, the rate and response to new issues increases; and that, when bear markets approach their bottoms, the volume in new-issue activity is extremely low. So the trends in new-issue activity are used as contrarian buy or sell signals, as a means for estimating the extremes of a primary or secondary trend.

Industry Trends

Technicians may follow the entire market or individual issues. But many also track entire industries, in the recognition that, at various times, a particular industry leads the market. This means that price and volume

$$\frac{B}{V} = R$$

B = volume in block trading
V = total volume
R = large block ratio

$$\frac{33,000,000}{148,000,000} = 22.3\%$$

FIGURE 6.6   Large block ratio.

changes within an industry group may anticipate the near future for the market as a whole.

Recognizing the cycles of industry influence within the market is another technical strategy. Technicians attempt to recognize signs that a particular industry is moving into or out of favor among investors.

Volume Percentage Change

Investors Daily ranks each listed stock by increases or decreases in daily volume. This is done in comparison to averages over the preceding 50 trading days. When volume moves significantly away from the 50-day moving average, the technician may interpret the change as an important technical indicator.

Example: One stock reports volume percentage change above 125 percent of the 50-day moving average, for three consecutive days. The technical analyst interprets this as a sign that investor interest and demand is on the rise.

Example: One stock's volume percentage change falls to 80 percent of the 50-day moving average for several days. The technician sees this as a sign that the stock is falling out of favor with investors, and that demand for shares is on the decline.

Cumulative Volume Index

Another volume test involves following the trend in net upside and downside volume, in a running total. This requires two steps:

1. Subtract the daily volume for declining issues from the daily volume for advancing issues.
2. Add the net volume to the prior day's cumulative total.

Use of the cumulative volume index requires interpretation. Technicians look for major shifts in volume trends, as indicators that overall price movement will occur. For example, when a bull market nears its peak, daily upside volume will be expected to increase, so that the cumulative total will grow at a rate greater than average. This will be reflected on a chart, and as the curve increases, the technician will interpret it as a sell signal.

VOLATILITY TESTS

Besides price and volume tests, technicians are concerned with volatility—the degree of stability in a particular stock or industry group.

A highly volatile stock—one that experiences wide price swings—is considered more speculative than one whose volatility is relatively small. Volatility is measured in comparison to the market as a whole, or based on its own one-year trading range.

Beta

Beta is the comparison of a stock's price movement tendencies, compared to the market as a whole. It can be applied only when a stock moves in the same direction as the market. If a stock moves in a contrary direction, there is no reaction, and beta is zero.

Example: The market grows over a one-year period at the rate of 2 percent:

STOCK PRICE MOVEMENT	BETA
Up 2% (same as the market)	1.0
Up 3%	1.5
Up 1%	0.5

A variation on beta is the test of relative strength of a stock. This is a measurement not against the market, but against a particular index. For example, the change in price of a stock or industry group is divided by changes in the DJIA or S&P 500 index. Beta, as a test of price stability in comparison to the "market," most often means the exchange index (all issues). Relative strength is a comparison between the stock or industry group and a selective index.

Volatility

The second test is the simple volatility measurement itself, or a comparison of a price range to the lowest price during a one-year period.

Example: A stock had a price range for the last 52 weeks between 31 and 38 per share. Its volatility is computed by dividing the range (7 points) by the low, resulting in a volatility factor of 22.6 percent.

A seven-point spread will not result in the same volatility factor for each issue. A higher-priced stock will show a lower degree of volatility for the same price spread.

Example: A stock's price range for the last year was between 79 and 86—seven points. Volatility for this period is 8.9 percent.

The formula for calculating volatility is shown in Figure 6.7.

Relative Price-Strength Ranking

A rating applied by *Investors Daily* to each listed stock measures volatility on a scale between 0 and 99. This relative price-strength measurement is compared to a 12-month period for each issue. A higher ranking indicates one of two things: a better than average price rise in a rising market, or a lower than average drop in a falling market. Thus, the ranking can be used to identify stocks that performed well in the immediate past.

Many additional technical indicators may be used by both professional investment managers and individual investors. The dependability of technical information as a way to time decisions or to anticipate future price movement must always be questioned. Perhaps the most reasonable approach is to recognize that hindsight always has limits; that the current price of stocks discounts historical information; and that many factors beyond price, volume, and volatility trends will ultimately affect future price movement.

In the next chapter, we will discuss the methods for applying technical information, through formula investing and charting.

$$\frac{H - L}{L} = V$$

H = high price
L = low price
V = volatility

$$\frac{38 - 31}{31} = 22.6\%$$

FIGURE 6.7   Volatility.

7

Applying Technical Indicators

Information reviewed in isolation has little meaning. But when put into the context of a trend, the same information expands our comprehension, and leads to better decisions.

This is the premise under which the technician operates. In the last chapter, some of the popular and closely monitored technical indicators were explained and illustrated. In this chapter, we will see how the technician interprets those indicators and puts them to use—through the study of chart patterns, by the use of moving averages for price movement trends, and by applications through formula investing.

There are many technical methods in use today, including some rather complex formulas involving two or more different indicators, used in conjunction, to develop patterns, forecasts, and trends. Our purpose is not to provide a comprehensive explanation of every possible technical strategy; rather, it is to demonstrate *how* technical information is applied to determine the timing of decisions.

Since the purpose of any form of analysis is to identify opportunities in the marketplace and to decide when to buy or sell securities, it is important to keep a perspective on why analytical efforts are put forth. In developing a procedure for analyzing and tracking securities and looking for emerging trends, there is a danger that the approach may become the end in itself.

Investors who become overly engrossed by the details of analysis may lose sight of their goal: to make profitable decisions through clear, well-focused selection and interpretation of facts. With this in mind, we will explain basic charting patterns and methods for developing trend averages; and then explain the mathematical aspects of commonly used formula investing techniques.

CHARTING PRICE MOVEMENT

The technical analyst may track a particular selection of indicators in order to identify opportunities, and to make decisions. Most of this effort is concerned with anticipating future price movements, and the tracking is achieved with the use of charting.

The investor who charts price movements believes in the predictability of the market, and rejects the Random Walk Hypothesis described in the last chapter. It is a contradiction to believe that price movement is completely random, and still respect the trends shown on stock charts. Yet many investors watch charts faithfully, while claiming to believe in the Random Walk. The two ideas are in conflict.

The technically inclined investor who constructs charts (or who subscribes to a service that supplies charts) believes that price movements are predictable within definite patterns. In addition, the belief is that patterns tend to repeat themselves on a recurring basis. Many theories about arithmetic and geometric attributes in price movement are similar to the Elliott Wave Theory—that is, a visible trend develops in the movement of a stock's price, making the future predictable.

Chartists depend on the patterns that develop in charts for the market or for individual issues, to identify directions in price movement. The complication arises in the fact that time is the uncertain factor. There is no way to know how long a pattern will take to develop. In fact, interpreting charts for future price movement is extremely difficult with the time factor involved. And making investment decisions without considering the timing implication is a useless exercise.

Most arguments favoring the use of charts involve a good deal of hindsight. A look backward easily reveals identifiable patterns in price movement, although at the time those patterns were developing, the meaning they represented might have been less certain.

You can use charting to your advantage by recognizing the basic principles underlying the science. Certain pattern attributes are worth examining, and an understanding of their significance may help in the timing of buy and sell decisions.

Support and Resistance Levels

The range in which a stock is trading is defined by top and bottom prices. At the top is the resistance level, defined as the maximum price at which investors are willing to buy or sell that stock, within a time range. At the bottom is the support level, which is the lowest price at which investors will buy or sell.

The resistance and support levels change over time, as price movement breaks away from the price range traded in a specific period. One way that this information can be applied in the timing of investment decisions is to identify the typical duration for which one set of price ranges exists. A stock, for example, might experience a resistance/support range for three months, after which the price tends to move to somewhat higher levels. By identifying this pattern, you may be able to better estimate and time the appropriate buying and selling opportunities. A range currently defined may advance or retreat in the future, perhaps in recognizable cycles.

Resistance and support are reflections of value cycles. Investors may perceive that a particular stock is worth a given average price this year; but next year, that perception could be increased a few points (or, given a changing market, it could as easily be decreased).

Figure 7.1 shows two versions of the resistance and support level. In the first version, the current levels are defined by the maximum range of prices during a limited period of time. In the second, a longer study of price ranges shows an advancing resistance and support range.

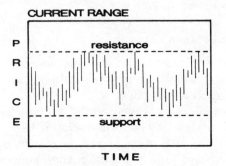

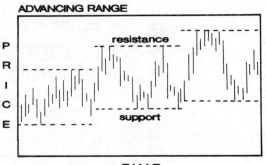

FIGURE 7.1 Support and resistance levels.

Breakout Patterns

When resistance and support levels remain intact on the chart, the stock is stable, within that range. But when the price extends above or below the levels, a breakout occurs.

Breakout patterns occur on the upside (bullish) as well as on the downside (bearish). When the resistance or support levels are broken through, however, it does not necessarily signal a permanent shift in those levels. The pattern could retreat back to original levels, or even continue in the opposite direction. Any study of charts will reveal as many false signals as dependable ones.

A true breakout often is accompanied by tests of the resistance or support levels in the period just before the breakout occurs. For example, a price level approaches the resistance level several times over a four-week period, finally breaking through. Some chartists will point to the repetitive tests as a sign that the breakout is probably a strong and permanent one.

This interpretation is often wrong, however. A resistance level may also be tested several times just before a breakout occurs—but not on the upside. (See the next section, double top and bottom patterns.)

Breakout patterns, both for upside (resistance) and for downside (support) changes, are shown in Figure 7.2.

Double Top and Bottom

When prices test resistance and support levels twice within a limited period of time—without breaking through—the pattern may anticipate a price movement in the opposite direction.

When the price falls successively to the support level, and that level holds, an upside breakout may occur in the immediate future. And on the opposite side, successive tests of a resistance level without breaking through may lead to a downward slide in prices, beyond support levels.

Double tops and double bottoms are illustrated in Figure 7.3.

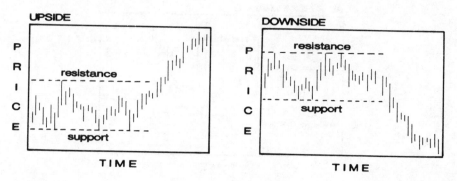

FIGURE 7.2 Breakout patterns.

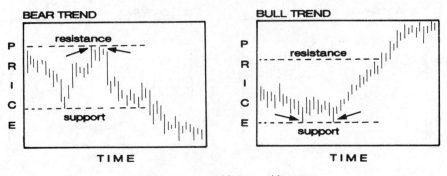

FIGURE 7.3 Double top and bottom.

Head and Shoulders Pattern

One of the common patterns that chartists point to is called the *head-and-shoulders*. This refers to a series of three up-and-down movements in price, the middle one being greater than the first and third (thus, the descriptive name).

The pattern anticipates a bearish movement in price, and runs in the following sequence:

1. The first "shoulder" occurs, consisting of a rise in price followed by a retreat.
2. The "head" occurs, in which the price again rises, but to a higher level than before. This is also followed by a retreat.
3. The third phase, another "shoulder," is similar to the first. However, the price continues moving downward.

The inverted head-and-shoulders pattern is bullish. Rather than a series of upward price movements followed by offsetting downward movements, the opposite occurs. The head and shoulders pattern is a form of bottom or top testing, followed by a breakout.

Both head-and-shoulder patterns are shown in Figure 7.4.

Gap Patterns

In certain situations, the opening price and trading range of a stock on one day will occur above or below the trading range for the previous day. This creates a gap in the chart.

There are three types of gaps:

1. Breakaway Gap: This is characterized by a price movement following the gap, well away from the previous trading range. For example, a stock

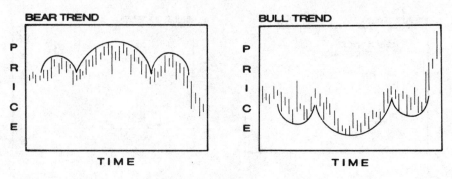

FIGURE 7.4   Head-and-shoulders.

is trading in a range between $30 and $35 per share. A breakaway gap occurs, with the stock trading between $37 and $40. The trend from that point forward is bullish, with prices progressing away from the previous trading range.

2. Runaway Gap: This form of gap usually occurs at a time of substantial price change, either upward or downward. The trend is generally one-sided, showing either a huge upward or huge downward movement. This will result from overly enthusiastic, even panic trading in one issue, and is accompanied by exceptionally heavy volume.

3. Exhaustion Gap: When a run-up or run-down of prices comes to an end, the exhaustion gap may occur. This is the "last gasp" of a substantial or sudden price change. It is characterized by a relatively stable price period, known as the island, and may precede a price movement in the opposite direction (the island reversal).

The three forms of gap are shown in Figure 7.5.

Volatility Formations

As a stock's price range broadens or narrows, meaning a change in the volatility of the issue, a triangular pattern will emerge. As price ranges broaden, the triangle expands as well. And as it narrows, so does the triangle.

Triangles may occur in short-term situations, but are difficult to pin down in patterns. In fact, over a period of time, any stock's price movements can be reduced to triangular shapes; however, the usefulness of that pattern is questionable.

When identifying volatility trends, the broadening and narrowing price ranges can serve as useful indicators. For example, for several months you have been interested in purchasing shares of one company's stock. However, you hesitated because the price range was overly volatile. In recent

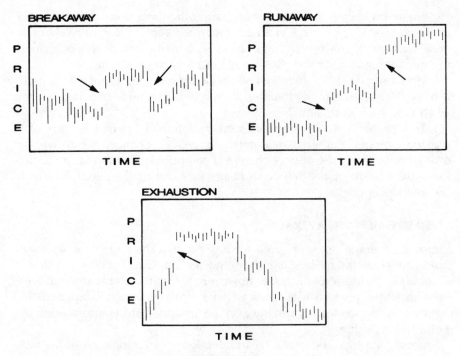

FIGURE 7.5 Gaps.

weeks, however, the range has narrowed. The price range appears to have "settled down" into a less volatile range.

Broadening and narrowing volatility patterns are shown in Figure 7.6.

Movement in price for any single day cannot be thought of as significant, even when it contributes to what you believe is a recognizable pattern. There are no certainties in charting. The best you can expect is to gain indications of probable future movement—all based on the assumption that prices and patterns do repeat and are predictable.

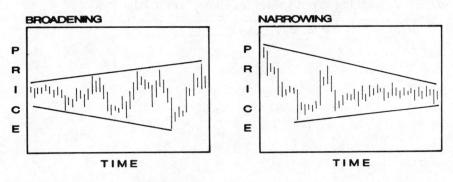

FIGURE 7.6 Volatility formations.

Singular changes in price, volume, and other factors must be analyzed in a larger context, before a trend can emerge. Even plotting price changes on a chart can be misleading, since an exceptionally high degree of change in one day tends to distort the average movement over time.

How can a trend be followed so that a broader significance is gained? If daily fluctuations are distracting, then of what value is charting, except as an exercise in hindsight?

This problem is partially corrected by following trends as part of a moving average. Rather than entering one day's change or one week's change on a chart, the *average* change is computed. This tends to modify the extreme movements that occur at any time during the period to which the average applies.

SIMPLE MOVING AVERAGE

A moving average can be figured for any period. The longer the average period covered, the more stable the trend will appear. Stability in a trend is not always a desirable feature, however. A highly volatile price movement should appear volatile, even when a moving average is applied. In that case, using too long a moving average actually distorts information or minimizes its value.

Moving averages are useful for tracking long-term trends, given the fact that daily and even weekly changes may be subject to seemingly large and distracting degrees of change. To follow a trend over a number of weeks, months, or even years, moving averages of long-term periods are not unusual.

For our purposes, we will demonstrate various methods of computing a moving average using a seven-day period. In practical applications, you may find that trends are more easily followed on a seven-week basis, with weekly changes employed in place of daily changes.

An average is computed by adding up the values in a specified field, and then dividing the total by the number of values involved. For example, the seven-day average on the seventh through the tenth days of a period will involve adding seven values, as shown in the table below.

DAY	VALUE			
1	47			
2	49			
3	46			
4	48	48.57		
5	49		49.29	
6	51			48.86	
7	50				49.29
8	52			
9	46			
10	49			

To compute an average, the field (range of values) is added together, and the sum is divided by the number of values in that field. However, to compute a moving average, a second step is required, as the average must progress to the subsequent period.

In the second step, the oldest value is dropped off, and a new value is added. In the example above, days 1 through 7 represented the moving average for the seventh day. To compute the same average for the eighth day, the total value of the field must be changed:

a) Reduce the field total by the value of the first day.

b) Increase the field total by the value of the eighth day.

Following this, the field is again divided by 7, the number of values in the field. This process is repeated for each subsequent day.

In working with moving averages for a large number of periods, it is important to check the total occasionally to ensure that no math errors have been made.

The formula for computing a moving average is shown in Figure 7.7.

$$1. \quad \frac{F}{D} = A$$

$$2. \quad \frac{F-1 + (F+1)}{D} = A$$

F = field
D = number of periods in field
$F-1$ = oldest day in field
$F+1$ = replacement day
A = moving average

$$1. \quad \frac{47 + 49 + 46 + 48 + 49 + 51 + 50}{7} = 48.57$$

$$2. \quad \frac{49 + 46 + 48 + 49 + 51 + 50 + 52}{7} = 49.29$$

FIGURE 7.7 Formula: Moving average.

WEIGHTED MOVING AVERAGE

One problem with the simple moving average is that equal weight is given to all values in the field. This means that, if prices were substantially different in the earlier phases of the field range, then the current average will not always reflect the true trend. Most investors will agree with the contention that later values are of greater significance in a trend than are the earlier ones.

This problem is offset by weighting the average. This can be done in a number of ways, some of which are made practical only when a computer program is available to aid in the calculations. For example, if you are working with a 200-day moving average, having to weight each value by a different factor will be tedious and impractical.

One form of weighted moving average involves increasing the relative value of each period, so that the latest period has the greatest degree of weight. Thus, the most dated values are reduced in relative impact as part of the formula; and the more current value factors have an increasing degree of weight. This method ensures that the latest changes have greater impact on the moving average.

Example: For a seven-day moving average, the divisor will be 28, representing the addition of the periods in use. Then, each period's relative weight is increased for progressive periods:

$$1 + 2 + 3 + 4 + 5 + 6 + 7 = 28.$$

Using the same values as in the simple moving-average illustration above, the weighting will be assigned so that the first day in the field has a value of 1; the second day has a value of 2; and so forth, until the seventh and most recent day has a value of 7:

		Seventh day		
DAY	VALUE	WEIGHT	TOTAL	AVERAGE
1	47	× 1	47	
2	49	× 2	98	
3	46	× 3	138	
4	48	× 4	192	
5	49	× 5	245	
6	51	× 6	306	
7	50	× 7	350	49.14

The same procedure is followed for computing the weighted moving average for the eighth day. The values used are days 2 through 8, and weighting is applied in the same manner:

		Eighth day		
DAY	VALUE	WEIGHT	TOTAL	AVERAGE
2	49	× 1	49	
3	46	× 2	92	
4	48	× 3	144	
5	49	× 4	199	
6	51	× 5	255	
7	50	× 6	300	
8	52	× 7	364	50.11

The ninth day:

		Ninth day		
DAY	VALUE	WEIGHT	TOTAL	AVERAGE
3	46	× 1	46	
4	48	× 2	96	
5	49	× 3	147	
6	51	× 4	204	
7	50	× 5	250	
8	52	× 6	312	
9	46	× 7	322	49.18

And for the tenth day:

		Tenth day		
DAY	VALUE	WEIGHT	TOTAL	AVERAGE
4	48	× 1	48	
5	49	× 2	98	
6	51	× 3	153	
7	50	× 4	200	
8	52	× 5	260	
9	46	× 6	276	
10	49	× 7	343	49.21

This procedure becomes increasingly cumbersome as the size of the average field increases, and as the number of periods to be calculated grows. An alternative procedure is to weight each period equally, except the latest one, which is given twice the weight of the others.

Example: Using the same values as above, the final day's value in each calculation is added twice; and the field is then divided by 8 instead of by 7:

Day 7		Day 8		Day 9		Day 10	
DAY	VALUE	DAY	VALUE	DAY	VALUE	DAY	VALUE
1	47	2	49	3	46	4	48
2	49	3	46	4	48	5	49
3	46	4	48	5	49	6	51
4	48	5	49	6	51	7	50
5	49	6	51	7	50	8	52
6	51	7	50	8	52	9	46
7	50	8	52	9	46	10	49
7	50	8	52	9	46	10	49
	390		397		388		394
	8		8		8		8
=	48.75	=	49.63	=	48.50	=	49.25

EXPONENTIAL MOVING AVERAGE

A final form of computation is the exponential moving average. This is simpler to compute than any other method, and also adds weight to the most recent values.

The exponential moving average calculation is especially practical when you are dealing with a long field of values, or when the moving average must be computed frequently. The calculation does not require a great deal of time to complete.

Before beginning to calculate, however, you must first determine the exponent (multiplier) for the field you will be using:

Formula: Exponent

$$\frac{2}{\text{Field}} = \text{Exponent.}$$

In our example, we have been using a field of seven days. Thus, the exponent is:

$$\frac{2}{7} = 0.29.$$

The steps involved in calculating the exponential moving average are:

Step 1: Calculate the simple moving average for the   Days 1 to 7
first period.   =   48.57

Step 2: Enter the next day's value.   Day 8 = 52

                                                              52.00
Step 3: Subtract the previous day's average from the   − 48.57
current value.   3.43

                                                               3.43
Step 4: Multiply the remainder by the exponent (round   × 0.29
to 2 places).   0.99

                                                               0.99
Step 5: Add the answer in step 4 to the previous   + 48.57
moving average.   49.56

These steps are repeated for each subsequent day in the period over which the moving average is calculated. When the difference between the calculated exponential moving average and the daily value is negative, the calculated fractional value is subtracted from the previous average, as shown in the table below. In this example, the moving average for day 7 is calculated under the simple moving average method; and days 8, 9, and 10 are calculated under the exponential method:

DAY	PRICE	PRIOR DAY	FACTOR	EXPONENT	NEW VALUE	E.M.A.
7						48.57
8	52	48.57	3.43	0.29	0.99	49.56
9	46	49.56	−3.56	0.29	−1.03	48.53
10	49	48.53	0.47	0.29	0.14	48.67

We have examined four different methods for computing a moving average. Obviously, the exponential method is the easiest to calculate, and it provides a desirable degree of weight to the later factors. The difficulty in calculating that is involved with the first three methods points to the desirability of the exponential method. A comparison of all four methods shows little variation in results for the short period used in our example:

DAY	SIMPLE	WEIGHTED	LATE WEIGHTED	EXPONENTIAL WEIGHTED
7	48.57	49.14	48.75	48.57
8	49.29	50.11	49.63	49.56
9	48.86	49.18	48.50	48.53
10	49.29	49.21	49.25	48.67

Ultimately, the value of moving averages is reflected on a chart. The technique removes the daily or weekly swings in value, and equalizes the longer-term trend. An example is shown in Figure 7.8, where both the daily values and moving averages are shown together.

FORMULA INVESTING

Most discussions of technical analysis are limited to the indicators other than financial information as explained in the last chapter, and the charting techniques demonstrated in this chapter. However, we will now expand on the definition by discussing technical *methods* that investors may use.

A method for making investment decisions requires two phases: first is the approach, which may be fundamental or technical, or a combination of both. Second is the action phase. Money is placed into an investment or removed from it.

Certain techniques for making investments, for diversifying a portfolio, or for protecting a basic position require a specific formula. Thus, the techniques are referred to as *formula investing techniques.*

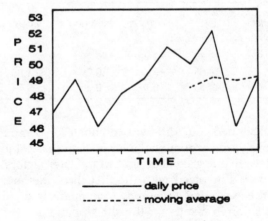

FIGURE 7.8   Moving average chart.

Constant-Ratio Plan

The first technique is one in which the investor establishes and then maintains a constant ratio between two or more different investments or types of investments. The distinction may be between the stock of two or more companies; between stocks and mutual funds; between stocks and bonds; or between two or more other groups.

The ratio can be applied in several environments. For example, one investor wants to apply a constant ratio formula between stocks and bonds, and practices this technique through a series of investments in mutual funds.

Example: You invest $40,000 in the market, and decide to apply a constant ratio rule. You will maintain 30 percent of your portfolio in a bond fund, and 70 percent in a stock fund. In the event your perception of the market changes in the future, you will change the ratio. A periodic review of your portfolio will dictate the need for modification, so that the ratio is maintained.

At the end of the first year, you make an additional investment of $5,000. This will be split in such a way that the constant-ratio rule is maintained:

	STOCK FUND	BOND FUND
Original Investment	$28,000	$12,000
Yield, one year:		
Dividends, 5%	1,400	
Interest, 7%		840
Total Value	$29,400	$12,840
Investment, $5,000	3,668	1,332
Total Value	$33,068	$14,172
Adjusted Ratio	70.0%	30.0%

This investment formula enables you to maintain your predetermined splits. As earnings accumulate, the ratio becomes distorted; and if subsequent investments are not made in consideration of the ratio, it will not be maintained.

For investors who cannot reinvest earnings, the constant-ratio plan is a simple one, to be modified only by appreciation in value.

Example: Instead of using stock and bond funds for the constant-ratio plan, an investor purchases stocks and bonds directly. Dividends and interest are paid out periodically, and placed in a money market fund.

In this case, the value of the original investment remains intact and earnings are placed elsewhere. So the basic ratio does not change. However, changes in the current market value of the holdings will change the ratio. Considering the commission rates for odd-lot trading, it is impractical to break a round lot of stocks or of bonds merely to maintain a constant-ratio plan.

Constant-Dollar Plan

A second formula is the constant-dollar plan, in which an investor determines in advance the amount that will be invested in one or more areas. For example, with total capital of $40,000 to invest, you might determine the following schedule in a constant-dollar plan:

1. $15,000 in stocks;
2. $10,000 in bonds;
3. $10,000 in balanced market funds;
4. $5,000 in money market fund.

When the maximum is exceeded, the excess is sold or transferred. And when market value falls, the difference is replaced. In the hypothetical four-part constant-dollar plan above, the $5,000 in the money market fund may be considered a variable. Earnings from the other three classifications are added to this amount; and if market value falls in any of the three groups, cash will be transferred from the money market fund to replace the loss.

Dollar-Cost Averaging

One formula requiring no periodic maintenance other than consistency is *dollar-cost averaging*. With this plan, the investor benefits from dips in market value.

With dollar-cost averaging, the average cost per share (or unit) will always be lower than the average price paid. This averaging effect is accomplished in one of two ways:

1. **Buying by the Share (or Unit):**   An identical number of shares is purchased at regular intervals, regardless of the per-share cost.
2. **Buying by the Dollar:**   The same amount is invested periodically, regardless of changes in the per-share cost.

An example of dollar-cost averaging under the constant-share approach: An investor buys ten shares in a mutual fund at the beginning of each month:

MONTH	SHARE PRICE	NUMBER OF SHARES	TOTAL INVESTED
Jan	$15.50	10	$155.00
Feb	16.01	10	160.10
Mar	14.92	10	149.20
Apr	15.10	10	151.10
May	16.35	10	163.50
Jun	17.01	10	170.10
Total		60	$949.00

To see the effect of dollar-cost averaging, divide the total invested by the number of shares purchased:

$$\frac{\$949}{60} = \$15.82.$$

An example of dollar-cost averaging under the constant-dollar approach: An investor deposits $150 per month in a mutual fund account:

MONTH	SHARE PRICE	TOTAL INVESTED	NUMBER OF SHARES
Jan	$15.50	$150.00	9.68
Feb	16.01	150.00	9.37
Mar	14.92	150.00	10.05
Apr	15.10	150.00	9.93
May	16.35	150.00	9.17
Jun	17.01	150.00	8.82
Total		$900.00	57.02

In this case, the average cost is computed by dividing the total invested by the number of shares purchased:

$$\frac{\$900.00}{57.02} = \$15.78.$$

Dollar-cost averaging reduces the risks of investment timing. Because future prices cannot be known in advance, the current price might be relatively high or relatively low. By making regular periodic deposits, the *average* cost will always be lower than the average price paid.

Technical analysis must be applied to your decision-making process with great care. A particular method of analysis might be simple or complicated, but the question each investor must answer is: How significant is the result the analysis produces? The importance of trends cannot be overlooked; and it is important to understand what a trend means, even more so than it is to develop a familiarity with the procedures for enacting a technical procedure.

In the next chapter, the combined use of fundamental and technical analysis will be examined—with an emphasis on the methods that must be put into effect to lead to informed decisions. That requires the proper identification of results, recognition of trends and their meaning, and ways to operate within a defined risk standard.

8

The Combined
Approach

A strong case may be made for fundamental or for technical analysis, based on the significance of the information revealed, *and* how it is used. However, that significance can be proved only in hindsight. The difficulty that every investor must face every day—even with the best information in hand—is deciding which indicators to use, and what conclusions to draw from it.

The fundamental school makes its argument by pointing to the past successes of financially strong companies. But the fundamental analyst also ignores the emotional character of the market as a whole. This is seen in the movements of averages, which overreact to news, or act in a manner contrary to popular logic.

The technical school is flawed by its preoccupation with trends and, in some instances, dependence on indicators that do not actually affect the price movement of the market, or of individual issues.

Recognizing these flaws, many investors conclude by using neither method exclusively. Rather, they select a limited number of fundamental and technical indicators, and use them together to study the market. With the huge number of possible approaches to take and methods to use, no one can possibly put to use every form of indicator. And if they could, the conflicting results would make the collective effort worthless.

The best approach to developing your own criteria for selecting investments is to first define your own risk standards. These may be expressed in terms of "acceptable" risks. That means a judgment must be made concerning volatility and recent price ranges and movements (technical indicators), as well as the company's financial strength, earnings, and competitive status (fundamental indicators).

ASSOCIATING CRITERIA WITH RISK

It would be difficult to imagine a comprehensively defined risk standard that did not include both fundamental and technical indicators. Even those who profess to act in the theories of pure fundamental or technical analysis will find themselves using ideas from the opposite school of thought.

> *Example:* A fundamentalist spends many hours studying the financial statements and trends reported in annual reports. However, recognizing that the Dow Jones Industrial Averages have risen to a five-year high, the same analyst is likely to proceed with caution, and will either withdraw a portion of invested funds, or hold off placing more money in a topped-out market.

In this example, a fundamentalist is forced to use a technical indicator. The DJIA is an index that tracks price movements in a limited number of issues. The idea that price movement is anything beyond random goes against the purely fundamental approach.

> *Example:* A technician tracks several stocks and narrows the field to four or five likely issues—all based on chart patterns for recent months. However, when it comes time to make a choice, the stock of a company in financial trouble is passed up.

In this case, the technician admits that in some situations, fundamentals may indeed play an important part. Although the entire premise of this investor's approach is to watch charts, when it comes time to decide where to invest money, the fundamentals rise to the surface.

Both disciplines offer something of value to the investor. But no matter what method anyone uses, he or she can only look to the past to judge the future. This imperfection is an integral fact of life in the market, and is one point that creates such excitement. The pure speculator, more than anyone else, recognizes that investing has much in common with gambling. Many gamblers have developed sophisticated systems for estimating the odds, and play accordingly—to an extent that many investment analysts would find impressive.

> *Example:* A roulette player watches the wheel and sees that the color red has come up on the last four turns. He reasons that black must come up next, and places a bet accordingly.

A chartist would agree with this strategy. The "odds" dictate that each color will come up approximately 50 percent of the time. Thus, it makes sense to expect the unusual trend to break. A fundamentalist, however, will point out that each spin is independent, and the results are not 50–50 collectively, but 50–50 each time.

Both points of view are valid, to a degree; yet neither is entirely correct because both are based on the past. In the end, the point of view each individual adopts is set by experience and then modified when a past experience is betrayed.

Example: A roulette player wins each time he places a bet on a color that has not come up in the last four turns. As a result, he concludes that the technique works. After applying this strategy several times, it stops working. So the player modifies his thinking, concluding that each turn is entirely random.

Example: An investor times the purchase and sale of stocks based strictly on chart patterns, and never bothers to read financial reports. This timing technique produces many profitable situations over a period of time. But then a string of poorly timed purchases results in a substantial loss. The investor reevaluates the technical approach, and begins paying attention to individual company financial information.

SETTING YOUR RISK STANDARDS

The only way to decide which fundamental or technical indicators to use is to first determine your own risk standard. Is the money you plan to invest essential to your financial plan? That is, can you *not* afford to lose it? On the other side, is that money purely for speculation purposes? Have you set it aside to risk, and can you afford to lose it? In between these extremes, you will find that risk exists in varying degrees, and changes as your financial condition changes, and as you gain investing experience.

Once you know your own degree of what investment professionals call "risk tolerance," you must next answer questions of analytical philosophy. Do you subscribe to the theory that market values rise and fall in predictable patterns? Or do you accept the Random Walk Hypothesis? Most investors find that they respect the technical science without fully accepting all of its premises. Thus, chart patterns are considered helpful but not conclusive. And financial analysis is useful in determining a company's strength, but does not always point the way to market demand and price.

The next question concerns the importance of the past. Since all forms of analysis must be based on historical information, how much weight should be given to each type of information that comes your way? Most analysts give much more importance to the most recent information, and assign ever-decreasing importance to older news.

> *Example:* An investor uses volatility as a means for selecting stocks, on the premise that a highly volatile stock is overly risky. However, this solitary test for selection is not dependable, because a stock's past record is not always indicative of future movements, nor of a given price range. Furthermore, a stock that moved dependably with the market in the past can unexpectedly move in the opposite direction, or even overreact to market trends.

There is no one method that can always be applied to the selection of investments. You must expect to have a degree of losses among the gains. The most successful investors are those who understand this principle, and who know their risks completely and can live with them. Certainly, no one wants to lose; but the realistic individual also knows that it's not possible to be right all of the time.

The answer to the selection dilemma is to develop a series of sensible criteria that results in timely decisions more often than in losses. With the exception of those stocks that perform exceptionally well or exceptionally badly, most stocks cannot be described as good or bad investments at any given moment. Rather, it's all in the *timing* of the decision.

> *Example:* With the use of a limited number of tests, an investor identifies several buy and sell signals, and makes decisions accordingly. A particular issue was especially attractive several months ago, and the investor purchased 300 shares. Today, though, the fundamental and technical indicators are negative. So the 300 shares are sold.

How many times have you heard this statement: "You should buy into this company. I bought shares last spring, and I've doubled my money." Obviously, that investor timed his decision well, as the result of either diligent analysis or pure luck. But the same stock might not be a good bargain today. In fact, if the rise in price is accurate, chances are the stock is now overpriced.

Perhaps the more important question is this: How many times have you acted, purely on the advice of others, and without any research of your own? Virtually every investor has taken this path at one time or another; the majority invest that way all the time. They respond to their fellow workers, relatives, or friends, or they take the advice of a stockbroker. Decisions are made without applying *any* analysis whatsoever.

This approach is all too common and, when analyzed, makes little sense. The investor who reacts to others is the most volatile, responding to sudden ups and downs in the DJIA, or to economic news. Such investors watch the technical indicators carefully, and yet they buy whatever someone else tells them to. Failing to perform analysis is a form of the Random Walk Hypothesis. Yet most investors defer to the judgment of someone else, while still watching the most widely known technical indicator of all. It may be said that in addition to often being wrong, the market is highly irrational.

One sure way to fail as an investor is to overreact on both sides of the decision. Buy without researching when someone else gives you a tip; and sell when the price tumbles, in a panic reaction to what the market is doing. If you invest in this way, you're just going along with the crowd, which is more often wrong than right.

You cannot know the future. But you can create an environment for making a very educated guess, once you define your risk standards and analysis criteria.

PREDICTING THE FUTURE

Even acknowledging that the procedure followed by most investors is illogical doesn't help the serious investor. After all is said and done, the problem still exists: How do you decide *what* to buy or sell, and *when* to act?

Many people consider investing a form of guessing the future; but remember that this is not the real purpose of performing analysis. The purpose must be to develop an intelligent method for minimizing losses, and for making the best possible decision today.

Chartists constantly try to interpret signals based on the visual patterns that come up in charts. Some even expand on this by applying various mathematical formulas to the charts to predict trends.

One popular theory of the market holds that you should never buy when a stock's price is falling, and that you should never sell while the price is rising. However, many faithful chart readers contradict this advice, pointing to the wave effect that often appears on their charts. Some stock prices, they point out, tend to move in a given price range, between the top and bottom.

There is a degree of validity in this observation, which can be explained by the supply and demand factors that rule the exchange market. As prices fall, an issue becomes more attractive; as a result, investors can purchase shares at bargain rates ("bargain" in this case defined as today's price, compared to the price in the past). And as prices rise, holders will want to take their profits.

These realities create the common wave pattern in the intermediate-term changes in stock prices. Of course, the overall market trend might dictate an upward or downward tendency in prices. The wave, though, will still manifest itself. So the chartist can certainly speculate by timing buy and sell decisions—once a wave pattern is established.

This technique will not always succeed, and there can be no guarantee that it will work even once. However, some investors have been able to time their decisions well enough to take short-term profits, and time purchases based solely on the up-and-down movements of prices within a few points.

Figure 8.1 demonstrates how these patterns work. As a stock's price bottoms, the chartist recognizes it as a buy signal—within a defined price range. And as it tops within the same range, that serves as a sell signal.

The interpretation problem is ever-present. A wave may establish itself and work for several weeks or months. Then, without any predictable reason or warning, the price pattern changes drastically. You cannot know in advance when or why this occurs.

An additional problem arises from the fact that, in hindsight, a pattern is obvious, but, at the moment you're studying a chart, the significance of the latest information is not always apparent. For example, at the time a stock's price is moving downward, you have no idea how far it will fall before turning around. And as it rises, you will not recognize the top until well after it has passed.

One of the pitfalls in depending solely on charts is that hindsight often is given too much weight. It's far too easy to look back and see *clear* signals, and far too difficult to interpret a chart today and recognize what it means for tomorrow.

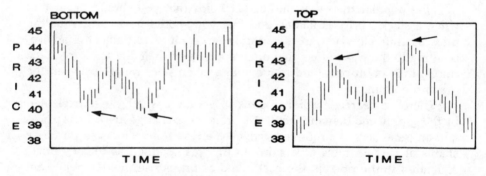

FIGURE 8.1 Predicting chart patterns.

OVERCOMING COMMON ERRORS

In determining a reasonable but limited number of tests to apply to your decision-making process, you must be aware of your risk standard in comparison to the inherent risks of the investments you select. You must also be aware of the mistakes that investors make repeatedly, and know how to avoid them. These include:

1. Selection of the wrong risk-level investment: When seeking high yields, investors tend to pick extremely volatile stocks. That translates to greater potential as well as to greater risks. In order for your decisions to work, they must be made in the context of a carefully defined risk standard.

Investors who are overly concerned about losses select stocks that are extremely conservative. Without any volatility to speak of, that stock's performance will be dull and potential profits in an up market will be lost.

2. Selection based only on price per share: Many investors believe that stocks with lower per-share prices are better bargains than higher-priced stocks. This perception is a misguided one. The cost per share, by itself, is meaningless. This should never serve as the basis for choosing stocks.

3. Poor timing on both sides: The classic description of the unsuccessful investor is one who buys when prices are high, and sells when they're low. As obviously wrong as that sounds, it's the way that the majority acts. When the market is climbing, people want to get in on the action, and this trend accelerates as the market gets closer to the top. And when the market falls, fear drives investors out of the market, a trend that peaks at the bottom.

4. Lack of patience: As part of the definition of your risk standards, you must determine whether you are in for the long term, or looking for a fast profit. Many investors never address this issue, and thus have no idea when they are supposed to close a position.

5. Lack of clear price goals: If you invest to make a profit as soon as possible, you must also define what you consider your price goal. Otherwise, you will not have any way of determining when to sell. In addition to a price goal on the way up, you should also set a bail-out point on the way down, which is the maximum loss you are willing to absorb. Once you reach either the price goal or the bail-out point, the position should be closed.

6. Indecision: Once you set clear goals for yourself, follow your own rules. Don't be an indecisive investor, or you will lose your potential profits and compound your losses. For example, your stock's price rises, but you hesitate because you think it might rise more. But instead, it falls below your original cost. At that point, you are still indecisive, because you want to recapture the lost paper profits. This cycle can repeat indefinitely.

7. Misguided motives: Be sure you know why you're investing. Don't sell before year-end just to create a loss you think you need for tax purposes, if that investment is still worth holding. And don't invest in speculative stocks just because the safer choices are not as exciting.

8. Investing from bias: Don't keep going back to the one investment in which you did well five years ago, unless it still meets your criteria. There is no logic in a misplaced sense of loyalty.

BUILDING YOUR CRITERIA

In developing your criteria for evaluating investments, you must be able to judge when to buy, hold, or sell. This means that the criteria you select must clearly indicate what to do—based on your judgment of the facts in hand.

In order for your criteria to work, you must be able to interpret and give significance to what you learn. So if you select criteria that produce nothing in the way of guidance, then the process is of no use. If your criteria do not prove accurate most of the time, you must question the validity of your selection basis.

The timing of decisions is the most critical point for every investor to keep in mind. So criteria must change over time, reflecting the dynamic changes occurring in the market, in the company in which you have invested, and in the market price and volume the stock is experiencing from one week to the next.

Your analysis can be performed on the market as a whole or on individual issues. For example, you can chart the advances and declines on the New York Stock Exchange; the daily new high/new low trend; the odd-lot balance index; and the large block ratio. These tests indicate the mood of the market. However, if you use these tests to time your purchase decisions for stocks that do not respond to market sentiment and movement, then there is no point to the exercise.

On the other hand, when your stocks react strongly with the changes in the overall market, those tests might prove to be worthwhile. Keeping in mind that the most logical way to approach the question of analysis is with a combination of fundamental and technical indicators, you must decide which indicators to follow. Here are some guidelines:

1. Seek mathematical ease: Avoid the task of having to undergo a complex series of equations each day. If you can perform analysis on an automated system, this solves the problem when you use the more complex methods.

2. Use outside services: Many useful broad-based tests are easily available, through the financial press (*Wall Street Journal* and *Investor's Daily*) on a daily basis. An excellent research service that provides ample fundamental and technical information for 1,700 stocks is the Value Line Investment Survey.

3. Limit your field: Don't overload yourself with so many different analytical tests that the process becomes unmanageable. Good analysis is quick and produces a clear indicator. Keep your field to ten indicators or less.

4. Abandon what doesn't work: Don't stay with a set of indicators if your timing and profit record does not improve as a direct result. Look for dependable but basic tests that give you trends and information you can count on.

5. Keep an open mind: Don't allow yourself to become an enthusiast for one method. And don't depend on the advice of one service or newsletter. Research constantly, and check into new procedures for analysis, even if they are contrary to your own premise.

> *Example:* One investor studied fundamental and technical analysis and settled on seven different indicators, with his own risk tolerance in mind. All of the information he used was available from the daily paper and from the Value Line Investment Survey. He tracked a list of several stocks on a weekly basis, and when one met his ranking criteria, he took that as a buy signal.

Each individual must decide on the indicators to use. We will show an example of how this system can work, complete with a typical ranking method. You may decide to replace the indicators used in the example with tests of your own preference, and to apply a ranking system that gives greater weight to a particular indicator.

Sample Analysis System

This is a sample of investment modeling, using seven indicators from the daily papers and the Value Line Investment Survey.

The seven tests selected are:

1. Price/earnings ratio;
2. Dividend yield;
3. Value Line timeliness ranking;
4. Value Line safety ranking;
5. Value Line industry ranking;

6. *Investor's Daily* earnings-per-share ranking;

7. *Investor's Daily* relative-strength ranking.

Value Line ranks each of the 1,700 stocks it tracks in terms of timeliness (1 is the most timely, down to 5, which is the least timely), and in terms of safety (1 is the safest, and 5 is the least safe). It also ranks major industries by overall strength and timeliness. *Investor's Daily* ranks each stock in relation to the rest of the listed market, for its EPS and relative-strength rankings.

In our investment model, the purpose of these seven tests is to identify stocks that represent timely investments and are superior choices. This system can be used to judge holdings as well as to determine when to sell.

Some potential problems with modeling of investments: If you attempt to analyze too many stocks, you will not narrow the field sufficiently to make a selection. Apply your test to fewer than ten stocks at any one time.

Another problem arises if you discover that none of the stocks you pick meets your criteria. This means that you are picking issues unsuitable for your risk standards; or that your standards are unrealistically high, to the extent that you find no qualified candidates. If this happens, evaluate both your risk standards and the types of issues you have selected.

Figure 8.2 shows a worksheet for investment modeling, using our seven sample indicators. At the end of each week, the applicable values, percentages or points are added for each stock in the appropriate column.

The next step is to compute the ranking itself. For this step, complete a selection-ranking worksheet like the one shown in Figure 8.3.

The number of points you give to each indicator level determines the relative weight of each. In this case, we have attempted to weight each of the seven at approximately the same level of significance.

A buy signal under this system could be at a point where a stock exceeds 14 points; and a sell signal might come up if a stock's rank fell to 10 or below. The ranking you actually assign must be modified, not only to alter the relative weight of the indicator, but to adjust your field so that a reasonable number of stocks rank above or below your middle range.

That's the ultimate test of a ranking field. If all of the stocks you pick fail the test, there's something wrong—either in the test or in the stocks selected. And if all of them pass the test, there is no real benefit in the selection, because no selection was made.

Ideally, most of the stocks you subject to your testing should be in the middle range. One or two should pass above your buy level in order for the test to work. The key is that a selection must occur, and it must be made on the basis of analysis that you take seriously.

Be cautious if your analysis process becomes overly complicated, or if the mathematical process itself becomes the focal point in your decision.

Investment Modeling Worksheet

Date _____

STOCK	(1) P/E	(2) DIV.	(3) T	(4) S	(5) IND.	(6) EPS	(7) RS

(1) Price/earnings ratio
(2) Dividend yield
(3) Value Line timeliness ranking
(4) Value Line safety ranking
(5) Value Line industry ranking
(6) Investor's Daily earnings per share ranking
(7) Investor's Daily relative strength ranking

FIGURE 8.2   Investment modeling worksheet.

While the mathematical process of investing is essential to true analysis, it is a means and not the end. The outsiders' view of a dedicated analyst often reveals a person who has lost sight of the original purpose, and has become intrigued with the challenge of prediction, rather than with the challenge of earning a profit.

It is very doubtful that you will ever meet someone who became a millionaire by investing without a dependable system. The system, however, is not the whole answer. Success in the market depends on diligence, intelligent research and testing, open-mindedness to new approaches and theories, and a mixture of *respect* with *doubt* for every form of analysis. Nothing works exclusively, and no one can predict the future with 100 percent accuracy. Investing success is hard work, but worth the effort. It should be enough to be able to make an informed decision and to gain a profit most of the time.

selection ranking

Stock _____ Date _____

	POINTS	RANKING
1. P/E ratio		
15 or below	plus 1	
16 or above	minus 1	_____
2. Dividend yield		
round to nearest whole number		_____
3. Value Line timeliness		
1 or 2	plus 2	
3 or 4	minus 1	
5	minus 2	_____
4. Value Line safety		
1 or 2	plus 2	
3, 4, or 5	minus 1	_____
5. Value Line industry ranking		
1 to 5	plus 3	
6 to 10	plus 2	
11 to 20	minus 1	
21 or higher	minus 2	_____
6. Investor's Daily EPS		
91 to 99	plus 3	
81 to 90	plus 2	
61 to 80	plus 1	
51 to 60	0	
36 to 50	minus 1	
35 or below	minus 2	_____
7. Investor's Daily relative strength		
81 to 99	plus 2	
61 to 80	plus 1	
41 to 60	0	
40 or below	minus 1	_____
total ranking		

FIGURE 8.3   Selection ranking.

9

Math for the Options Market

Few specializations in the investment industry are as involved with mathematics as the options market. An option is an intangible product, a contract rather than a form of ownership. And because options have a finite life, the question of value is unavoidably tied to the factor of time.

It is often said that anyone participating in options is not truly an investor, but a "player." This point of view claims that an investor must hold equity (through purchasing stocks, for example) or lend money (by buying bonds). Less respect is paid to the individual who leverages available capital through the options market.

However, just because options are not tangible does not mean that the option investor is not a legitimate and serious investor. Participants in this market are considered reckless speculators, willing to assume an unlimited degree of risk in the hope of gaining huge profits. These points of view come from a lack of understanding about the options market—largely the result of the complex mathematical issues and terminology inherent in the market.

OPTION TRADING

Options are contracts related to the future purchase or sale of stock. Every option contract exists for 100 shares of stock, and may be a call or a put.

A *call* is the right to purchase 100 shares of stock before a specified expiration date in the future. Each contract refers to a specific (or *underlying*) stock, and also specifies the price at which the shares will be purchased (also called the *striking price*).

A *put* is the right to sell 100 shares of stock under the same conditions. An individual who holds a put contract, also known as the option buyer, can exercise the option by the expiration date, and by so doing, may sell 100 shares of stock at the striking price.

131

Exercise is only one choice the option buyer has. That same option can actually be treated in one of three ways, each affecting the yield and risk in the transaction:

1. Exercise: When an option owner exercises an option, 100 shares of stock are purchased at the striking price. Exercise will take place when the current market value of the underlying stock is greater than the striking price (of a call), or lower than the striking price (of a put).

2. Cancellation: A buyer may sell the option at any time after purchase and before the expiration date. This will occur in one of two conditions: First, when the value of the option increases enough so that a profit exists, the option purchaser sells and receives proceeds greater than the amount invested. Second, if the value remains at or below the purchase price, and the expiration date is near, the purchaser may sell to get back the current market value.

3. Expiration: If the purchaser takes no action by the expiration date, the option ceases to exist. It expires worthless, and the entire amount invested is lost.

Options have several special features that do not exist in most other markets: An investor can act in a highly speculative manner and assume very great risks. This is the image most often associated with options. However, options can also be extremely conservative. It all depends on whether the investor assumes the position of a buyer or of a seller. And when acting in the role of seller, it depends on whether the investor *owns* the underlying stock, or does not.

There are several reasons for becoming involved with options, but there are only five basic techniques. They are:

1. Buying calls: A call grants the purchaser the right to buy 100 shares of the underlying stock. That right becomes more valuable if, before expiration date, the market value of the stock becomes greater than the striking price of the option.

Most buyers never intend to exercise their options. They hope the market value will rise, because that will mean a corresponding rise in the value of the option. If that occurs, the option can be sold at a profit.

This profit can be substantial, often as much as 100 percent or more, and can be achieved in a very short period of time—often in only a few days. However, the potential for extremely high profits can be enjoyed only by assuming a high risk as well. If the value of the option does not increase, it will become progressively worth less money. Thus, many option buyers sell and receive only a portion of their original investment, or allow their calls to expire worthless.

2. Buying puts: A put buyer hopes that the market value of the underlying security will fall. If this occurs, the value of the put will rise in a corresponding manner. But if the stock moves upward, or remains within a limited trading range, the put will lose value by the expiration date.

3. Selling calls (uncovered): This is the strategy that involves the greatest degree of risk. A seller, or writer of calls, grants the contractual right to someone else, a buyer. So if the stock rises substantially, the seller will have to deliver 100 shares of the stock at the striking price—no matter how high the market value rises.

> *Example:* An investor sells a call with a striking price of $40 per share. By the expiration date, the stock has a market value of $55 per share. The seller must purchase 100 shares at current market value, and then deliver them to satisfy the exercised option, meaning a sale at $40 per share. This transaction will involve a loss of $1,500.

The uncovered call seller receives the proceeds from selling the option (called the premium). However, the risk is unlimited because the market value could rise to an indefinite level by expiration date.

4. Selling calls (covered): A second method for selling calls is the most conservative option strategy. A *covered* call is one that is sold when the seller also owns 100 shares of stock. Thus, in the event of exercise, the shares are available to honor the option. Rates of return for covered call writing may average 30 percent or more per year.

The covered call writer may enjoy a consistent rate of return, but may have to give up profits from investing in stocks. In the event a stock rises substantially, and an open option is exercised, the shares must be delivered at the agreed-upon striking price.

5. Selling puts: A put cannot be covered in the same way that a call is covered. Taking a short position in stock and a short position in a put at the same time is a form of coverage. And by selling and purchasing puts at the same time, the short side of the position is hedged. The risk in selling puts, in comparison to covered calls, is relatively limited, because a stock's value cannot go beyond zero. Thus, if the striking price of an option is $25 per share, and the seller receives $300 for selling one put, the maximum risk is $2,200 (the striking price, minus the put premium paid to the seller).

In all options, the premium (amount received or paid for the contract) relates to 100 shares of stock. When that premium is $300, it is described simply as a premium of 3.

Investors buy options to leverage their capital, and in return they risk not realizing a profit by the expiration date. For example, you have the choice of buying 100 shares at $40 per share, or of buying a call for 3 (a premium of $300). If the stock rises to $50 per share, both the stock purchaser and the option buyer will realize a 10-point profit. However, the stock purchaser had to invest $4,000; the option investor needed only $300.

Investors sell options in the realization that time is on their side. Because every option will expire within a few months, the premium value will deteriorate between the transaction date and the expiration date.

THE OPTION'S DELTA

Option investors must be aware of the mathematical relationship between changes in the price of the underlying stock, and changes in the value of the option premium. The dynamics of this ratio will ultimately affect the profit or loss to be realized from the trade.

This ratio, called Delta, varies based on the current market value of the stock in comparison to the option's striking price. It is also affected by the current market perception of the stock, and how it is expected to move in the near future.

When the option changes in value point for point with changes in the value of the underlying stock, the Delta is at 1.00. Option investors know that when the Delta is higher or lower, it acts as a signal for timing the purchase and sale of options.

The typical Delta relationship depends on the distance between the market value and the striking price. When the condition is "at the money" (meaning the current market value of stock is identical to the striking price of the option), the Delta is normally about 0.80, meaning that the option premium changes at a rate equal to 80 percent of the change in the stock.

When the condition is "in the money" (current market value of stock is greater than the striking price of a call, or lower than the striking price of a put), the option is expected to move at a Delta of 1.00 or higher. It will be higher when market perception is optimistic for the stock (affecting Delta for calls) or especially pessimistic (for puts).

> *Example:* A rumor surfaces that a takeover offer is about to be announced, at a price per share well above current market value. That company's stock rises four points, and the related call option's premium value jumps six points—a Delta of 1.50.

When the condition is "out of the money" (below the striking price for calls, or above the striking price for puts), the Delta will be much lower. The farther out of the money, the lower the Delta—thus, the less an option's premium will react to stock price movement.

This is critical information. Option buyers need to see changes in the premium value in order to realize a profit before expiration; and sellers depend on deterioration in premium value for the same reason. These factors force purchasers to be attracted to options whose striking price is close to the current market value. Only then can the Delta be high enough to effect a profitable move in premium value.

Sellers have a similar dilemma. They receive the greatest amount of premium proceeds when option striking prices are close to the money. And the premium will be lower when far out of the money.

Delta is illustrated in Figure 9.1. In this example, the underlying stock moves up four points. If the option's premium also rises by four points, the Delta is 1.00, and if the option exceeds a four-point rise, the Delta will be at 1.50 (six points) or 2.00 (eight points). If the option reacts to the market-value change with an upward movement below four points, the Delta is fractional. A three-point move, for example, represents a Delta of 0.75.

Delta is an ever-changing factor in the options market. While certain high-profile stocks may involve a Delta pattern that reflects a lot of investor interest, the Delta cannot be consistently depended upon or predicted. Thus, the option investor must analyze Delta to seek windows of opportunity.

To compute Delta, divide the movement in the option premium by the movement in the stock:

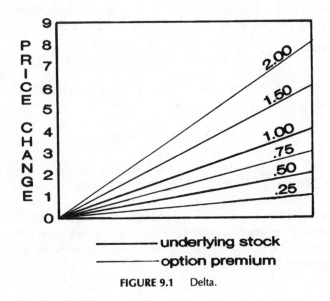

FIGURE 9.1   Delta.

Formula: Delta

$$\frac{O}{S} = D,$$

where

O = Change in the option premium,
S = Change in the stock's market price,
D = Delta.

Example: A stock's price rises by four dollars per share, while the related call's premium increases by only three dollars. Delta is:

$$\frac{3}{4} = 0.75.$$

INTRINSIC AND TIME VALUE

An option's Delta is further affected by the time remaining until expiration. Part of every option's value is called *time value*, representing that portion of the premium above any in-the-money premium. The total premium, minus time value, is called *intrinsic value* of the option.

Example: A call option is currently worth 4 ($400). The striking price is $35 per share, and the current market value of the stock is $36 per share. Intrinsic value of the call is simply the amount by which the current market value exceeds striking price:

$$36 - 35 = 1.$$

Time value is the difference. The option is worth 4 ($400), and intrinsic value is 1 ($100). Thus, time value is:

$$4 - 1 = 3.$$

For a put, the opposite is true. Intrinsic value is the amount by which current market value of the stock falls below the striking price.

Example: A put has a striking price of $35, and the current market value is $32 per share. A put has a current market value of 5 ($500). Intrinsic value is the difference between the striking price and current market value *below* it:

$$35 - 32 = 3.$$

Time value is the difference. The put is worth a total of 5 ($500), and intrinsic value is 3. Thus, time value is computed as:

$$5 - 3 = 2.$$

Formulas for intrinsic value and time value are:

Formula: Intrinsic value (calls):

$$MV - SP = I,$$

where
> MV = market value,
> SP = striking price,
> I = intrinsic value.

Formula: Intrinsic value (puts):

$$SP - MV = I,$$

where
> SP = striking price,
> MV = market value,
> I = intrinsic value.

Formula: Time value:

$$P - I = T,$$

where
> P = premium,
> I = intrinsic value,
> T = time value.

Whenever the current market value of the stock is lower than the striking price (for calls), or higher than the striking price (for puts), there can be no intrinsic value. And when the market value is identical to the striking price of any option, intrinsic value is also zero. In these cases, because intrinsic value is zero, the entire amount of the premium represents time value.

Example: A call is worth 3, and has a striking price of 35. The stock is currently selling at $34. Because the option is out of the money, there is no intrinsic value. The entire premium is time value.

Example: A put is worth 2, with a striking price of 40. The stock is now trading at $44. Because the current market value is higher than the striking price, the put is out of the money. The entire premium represents time value.

Example: An option has a striking price of 50, and the stock is currently trading at $50 per share. This option is at the money; thus, there is no intrinsic value. The entire option premium represents time value.

Intrinsic and time values, both for calls and for puts, are shown in Figure 9.2.

CALLS:

stock price	striking price	total value	intrinsic value	time value
34	35	4	0	4
37	35	2	2	0
40	40	3	0	3
43	40	4	3	1
42	45	3	0	3
45	45	1	0	1
48	50	4	0	4
56	50	6	6	0
49	55	2	0	2
53	55	7	0	7

PUTS:

stock price	striking price	total value	intrinsic value	time value
34	30	2	0	2
37	40	5	3	2
40	40	3	0	3
43	40	1	0	1
42	45	4	3	1
45	45	2	0	2
48	45	2	0	2
56	50	4	0	4
49	50	4	1	3
53	55	4	2	2

FIGURE 9.2   Intrinsic and time value.

Note the application of the formula. In the case of calls, intrinsic value can exist only when the current stock price is *greater* than the striking price (in the money). When the current stock price is below that level, there is no intrinsic value. In the case of puts, intrinsic value exists only when the current stock price is *less* than the striking price.

CHANGES IN TIME VALUE PREMIUM

By tracking the deteriorating time value of an option, you will see how the pending expiration becomes the most critical factor in the timing of option transactions. Time value falls at an accelerating rate as the expiration date approaches, so that by expiration day, nothing remains but intrinsic value.

This means that time is on the side of the seller. This is always the case. The greater the deterioration in an option's value, the more profitable the short position.

Example: An investor sells a covered call and receives a premium of 6 ($600). There are five months remaining until expiration. At the time the option is sold, the current market value of the stock is one point in the money. Two months before expiration, the stock is three points in the money, but the option's premium has deteriorated to 4 ($400). The investor closes the position by buying the option, and realizes a profit of $200.

If the same investor had *bought* the option under the same circumstances, a profit would not have been possible. That's because time works *against* the buyer. Even though the underlying stock rose two points higher than at the point of the transaction, time value fell.

Figure 9.3 demonstrates how this typically works. In this example, the stock and option are tracked at half-month intervals over a five and one-half month period (11 intervals). A July 40 call is involved, and the stock's value ends up at the money. Time value declines at a fairly regular series of steps, accelerating toward the end of the option's life. As of expiration date, there is no time value remaining.

This example assumes no unusual situations in the stock. For example, a rumor that the company might be a likely takeover candidate could increase time value above the "normal" course of decline. On the other hand, an unusually poor earnings report could accelerate the decline in time value, to below the expected levels.

A close review of the relationship between time value and intrinsic value reveals the importance of Delta. Whenever the Delta is above or below a normal range during a trading period, time value will be affected and opportunities will present themselves. There is a tendency for Delta aberrations to correct before expiration date. So by tracking change at various striking prices to market-value levels, those temporary changes can be identified.

Example: Using the chart in Figure 9.3, let's assume that at the end of the second month, a rumor hit the market that an offer would be made to acquire a controlling interest, at $45 per share. In that case, the stock would be likely to approach that level, based only on the rumor. Within a few days, the company may deny the rumor, and the stock's price would settle back to its previous level.

EXAMPLE: JULY 40 CALL

stock price	total premium	intrinsic value	time value
41	5	1	4
42	6	2	4
41	5	1	4
40	4	1	3
38	3	0	3
39	4	1	3
37	2	0	2
39	3	1	2
43	4	3	1
42	2	1	1
40	0	0	0

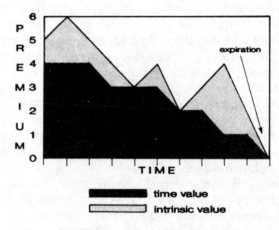

FIGURE 9.3   Time-value premium.

In reaction to the news, the option might act very differently from the stock. For example, if the stock rises four points, and the option goes up by five points, what does that mean? The Delta is 1.25, when the expectation, or "normal" in-the-money Delta, should be 1.00 only. For the seller, this Delta change presents a selling opportunity. Chances are, the Delta level will settle back down, meaning the premium is rich.

For a buyer, the opposite would be true. A Delta above 1.00 when in the money would mean it is a time to sell, not to buy. However, if the stock rose four points, and the option went up only three, then the Delta would be 0.75, or lower than the expected levels. This could be interpreted as a buy signal, assuming that the Delta later corrects.

Each option investor will interpret changes in the Delta according to his own rules. Some might attach no significance to aberrations in response to takeover rumors, for example; others may call the change normal under those conditions. However, as a general rule, it is possible to anticipate option premium changes in response to movement in the stock, at various positions related to striking price. When the Delta does not conform to that expectation, it usually represents an opportunity for the aware investor.

ROLLING TECHNIQUE

At the point where an option transaction is initiated, the selection must be based on thorough comparisons between the three possible outcomes. However, once a position has been opened, changes in value—both of the option premium and of the underlying stock—may dictate a change in strategy.

Options can be cancelled by way of an exchange for a new option. This is called *rolling* the option. Rolling can occur in a number of ways:

1. Rolling forward: The most likely action involves trading a current option for one with a later expiration date. This will be done when there is more time value in the later option, and for the purpose of avoiding exercise and increasing income.

> *Example:* You write a covered call and receive a premium of 5 ($500). Two months later, the stock has risen above the striking price and the option is now worth 7. To avoid exercise, you buy the original contract and sell a later one with the same striking price, for 9 ($900).

2. Rolling down: You may exchange an existing option for one with a lower striking price. However, in the event of exercise, this means you will have to sell 100 shares for a lower amount.

This may be worthwhile in a situation where the stock's market value declines after an option has been written, but when the basis is still lower than the revised striking price.

Example: You own 100 shares of stock that were originally purchased at $43 per share. Several months ago, the stock was valued at $52. At that time, you sold a call with a striking price of 55. Now, though, the market value is $49. You close the original option and replace it with one that has a striking price of 50.

Even when the stock's value has not fallen substantially, a roll down could make sense. For example, when the premium you will receive more is greater than five points above the value of a previous option, you are ahead in the event of exercise.

Example: You have sold an option with a striking price of 40, which is currently worth only 2 ($200). The stock's market value is now $38 per share. The 35 option is worth 8, which is six points more than the option you now hold. By rolling down, you give up five points in the event of exercise; but you gain six points from the exchange.

3. Rolling up: One option may be exchanged for another with a higher striking price but the same expiration date. This is one way to avoid exercise and to partially offset a loss.

Example: You sold an option with a striking price of 30, and the stock is now worth $33 per share. In order to avoid exercise, you close the original position and replace it with an option whose striking price is 35. In the event of exercise, you will sell 100 shares for five dollars more per share.

In this case, you may lose a portion of the income earned when you sold the first option. However, that may be justified by the five-point gain in exercise price.

Example: Your original option generated a premium of 5 ($500). It is now valued at 8, and the new option is worth 6:

First option sold	+500
First option closed	−800
Second option sold	+600
Net Income	+300

4. Rolling forward and up: The rolling technique can be combined. By rolling forward and up, you not only avoid exercise, but gain additional income from the greater time value of an option that has more time before expiration.

> *Example:* A covered call is currently valued at 9 ($900). It was originally sold for 6. It can be closed and replaced with a later option that also has a higher striking price; the premium is identical, 9:

First option sold	+600
First option closed	−900
Second option sold	+900
Net Income	+600

5. Rolling forward and down: The same technique can be applied when the underlying stock has fallen below the striking price. An original option can be exchanged for a later one with a lower striking price. This is worthwhile when the greater time value makes the replacement contract worth more than five points of difference.

> *Example:* The option you sold several months ago had a striking price of 50, and generated $800 in premium income. The stock is now worth only $47, and the option has declined to 3 ($300). However, an option with a later expiration date is worth 9 ($900):

First option sold	+800
First option closed	−300
Second option sold	+900
Net Profit	+1400

The rolling technique is made profitable when taking advantage of time values in contracts with later expiration dates. In theory, one option could be rolled forward and up indefinitely. However, exercise could occur at any time that an in-the-money condition exists.

This technique can be applied when you own more than 100 shares of stock, by incrementally increasing the number of contracts sold at any one time. For example, let's assume that you own 400 shares of stock, and you write one call when the stock is valued just below $30 per share. Then, over the next few months, the market value of your stock gradually increases to $45 per share. It will be possible to roll forward and up to avoid exercise, and still build in the increased market value. Thus, in the event of exercise, you will sell 400 shares not at $30 per share, but at $45 per share:

	OUTCOME
1. Sell 1 Jul 30 call at 4	$ +400
2. Buy 1 Jul 30 call at 6	−600
Sell 2 Oct 35 calls at 4	+800
3. Buy 2 Oct 35 calls at 5	−1,000
Sell 3 Jan 40 calls at 4	+1,200
4. Buy 3 Jan 40 calls at 7	−2,100
Sell 4 Apr 45 calls at 5	+2,000
Net Premium	$ 700

The commission cost included in this series of transactions will be substantial—from $300 to $600 or more, depending on your broker's fee policies for option transactions. This example illustrates the *principles* of rolling techniques, but commission costs must be considered before executing the strategy—or the objective to be realized must be studied on the basis of net amounts realized *after* fees.

To review all five forms of rolling technique, study the summarized option listing chart below:

| STRIKING | | PREMIUM | |
PRICES	JUN	SEP	DEC
40	7	8	10
45	2	3	5
50	1	2	4

Each technique can be developed based on this chart, assuming you hold one covered call with the June 45 striking price:

1. **Rolling forward:** Exchange Jun 45 for Sep 45 or for Dec 45

2. **Rolling down:** Exchange Jun 45 for Jun 40.

3. **Rolling up:** Exchange Jun 45 for Jun 50 (in this case, you lose one point in the option, but gain five points in potential exercise).

4. **Rolling forward and up:** Exchange Jun 45 for Sep 50 or for Dec 50.

5. **Rolling forward and down:** Exchange Jun 45 for Sep 50 or for Dec 50 (the greater time value offsets the potential loss of five points in exercise level).

COMBINED STRATEGIES

There are only five basic option trades: buying calls, buying puts, selling uncovered calls, selling covered calls, and selling puts. However, these can be combined in many ways.

Some of the advanced option strategies can become quite confusing, since they may involve multiple contracts, hedged ratios, and uncertainty about risk levels. Our purpose in this section is to demonstrate how a risk can be reduced to an understandable level.

Option strategies might look very safe on paper, but could hold the potential for greater risks than you realize. For this reason, a combination strategy should be mapped out and analyzed at various levels of market value for the underlying stock. In this way, you will be able to identify price ranges of limited and unlimited loss potential.

There are three broad classifications of combination strategy:

1. **Spreads:**   A spread is the simultaneous purchase and sale of options on the same underlying stock, with different striking prices, different expiration dates, or both.

   A *vertical* spread describes a situation in which striking prices are different, but expiration dates are identical.

   A *horizontal* spread involves the same striking price but different expiration dates.

   A *diagonal* spread is one in which both striking price and expiration date are different.

2. **Straddles:**   Straddles involve the simultaneous purchase and sale of the same number of option contracts, one side made up of calls and the other of puts. Striking price and expiration date are identical.

3. **Hedges:**   A hedge is any strategy in which one position protects against the risks inherent in another. For example, owning 100 shares of stock hedges the risk of selling a call.

To demonstrate how a combined strategy should be reduced to a form in which proper analysis can be performed, we will study a ratio calendar spread. This involves selling and buying an unlike number of options, with different expiration dates.

Example: You enter into a ratio calendar spread in which you sell 4 Jul 40 calls, each for 3 (producing income of $1,200); you also buy 2 Oct 40 calls for 5 each (costing $1,000). The net income before brokerage fees is $200. Now, the question becomes: What is the degree of risk or profit potential at various market values of the underlying stock?

Actual out-of-pocket for these transactions will be greater if you
don't have other securities in your portfolio, to pledge as collateral.
Your brokerage firm will place a margin call on your short position.
For the purpose of this illustration, we're assuming that collateral
is in the account.

To determine the answer, you should prepare a worksheet that summarizes the profit or loss from each position. Since you receive three points
for each call sold and the striking price is 40, the $43 level is a breakeven
point. If the stock is valued at 43 and the option is exercised, you will break
even (before brokerage fees). For calls that were purchased, the breakeven
does not occur until the underlying stock reaches a price of $45 per share
(since they cost 5 each). This form of analysis must assume exercise or
cancellation without any consideration for time value. A judgment about
the risk of an option strategy should be done only on the basis of intrinsic
values:

	Analysis		
STOCK	PROFIT OR LOSS		
PRICE	JUL 40	OCT 40	TOTAL
50	− 2800	1000	− 1800
49	− 2400	800	− 1600
48	− 2000	600	− 1400
47	− 1600	400	− 1200
46	− 1200	200	− 1000
45	− 800	0	− 800
44	− 400	− 200	− 600
43	0	− 400	− 400
42	400	− 600	− 200
41	800	− 800	0
40	1200	− 1000	200
39	1200	− 1000	200

The pattern of risk and potential gain is established by preparing this
worksheet. This demonstrates that, in the event the market value of the
underlying stock rises, the risk increases by 2 ($200) for each point. This
represents the net difference between selling four contracts and buying
two. At the same time, the maximum profit potential is the amount of
premium already received, or $200. If, however, the earlier calls—which
were sold—were to expire worthless in July, you would still own the two
calls purchased, which do not expire until October.

From this analysis, you can see that the risk exists between the transaction date and expiration of the earlier calls. After that point, any increases

in the value of the underlying stock will produce profits in the Oct 40 call positions.

An analysis of risk that is done visually, as is the example above, helps clarify the decision for you. It is not enough to understand the concept of risk; you often must be able to see it on a worksheet in order to comprehend the degree of risk involved in a strategy. With certain option techniques, you might discover that the exposure is greater than what you're willing to bear.

This is the reason that a careful analysis must be performed. Options can be highly speculative and risky, or extremely conservative and profitable. Before proceeding with an option strategy, be certain that you understand the risks involved. Also be sure you set rules for yourself, restricting the degree of risk you are willing to take; and then follow those rules.

By applying the mathematical knowledge concerning shifts in Delta, and by learning to use time value to your advantage, you can make options a source for profits (notably, using the covered call technique). Or, with a limited portion of your portfolio, you may leverage capital to purchase options, based on a study of market sentiment and timing of decisions.

10

Math for the Bond Market

Evaluating yield is a fairly straightforward estimate for most investments. However, bond investors are faced with the question of evaluating their returns in a number of different ways, based not on estimates but on known information.

Even though bond yields are fixed, it may prove difficult to identify exact yield, for several reasons:

1. Market value of the bond itself may change frequently and substantially, based on the changing conditions in the financial markets.

2. Returns often are compared to assumed rates that can be earned in other bonds, or in investments other than bonds. If the assumption is flawed, the estimate will be flawed as well.

3. A true rate of return must include calculations for the time value of money. Thus, a thorough analysis will be quite involved.

4. Discounts from face value and premiums paid above face value must be accrued or amortized to arrive at a true rate of return. This involves a complex series of calculations for each semiannual period.

The challenge is to arrive at a dependable and fair method for *comparing* bonds to one another, or to other investment choices. You may conclude that it is not necessary to identify a specific rate of return; it may be enough to simplify the process of comparison.

VALUE OF DISCOUNTED BONDS

Bonds can be purchased through mutual funds, unit investment trusts, or at a substantial discount. Zero coupons, first made available in the early 1980s, actually are stripped coupons. Investment firms strip coupons from bonds and sell those coupons at present value. Rather than paying interest each year, the deeply discounted bond makes only one payment in the future, at face value.

Because discounted bonds are purchased at a fraction of face value, many investors who used to stay out of this market can now participate with minimal capital. The amount of investment required depends on two factors:

1. The time remaining until maturity.
2. The interest rate.

Our first formula deals with the present value of a bond. You must be able to calculate this in order to evaluate a discount bond, and to determine the cost of purchasing one. The questions to be addressed are:

1. How long a period will be required for the discounted bond to mature?
2. What is the interest rate?
3. How much must be deposited today?

Most purchasers of zero coupon and other discount bonds, not knowing how to perform this calculation, must call an investment company and ask for yields. Thus, there is little opportunity to evaluate the bond before calling to place an order.

Example: You are considering purchasing a zero coupon bond in your retirement plan. Your target retirement date is 20 years away. You are interested in finding a bond that will mature in 20 years, and you will need to know the cost per bond, given available interest rates. You also want to know the rates applicable to 10-year and 15-year bonds.

To calculate the cost, it will be necessary to figure out the present value of the bond. To do so, divide the face value ($1,000 per bond) by the interest rate that will be applied each half-year (bond interest is paid semiannually, so the calculation will always be done on that basis).

A 20-year discount bond, yielding 10 percent, will require a deposit today of $142.05. That bond, upon maturity, will be worth $1,000.

There are two ways to calculate this, using present-value tables:

1. Use the present value at 10 percent for 20 years, as reported on the semiannual compounding table.

2. Use the present value at 5 percent for 40 years (periods), as reported on the annual compounding table.

The factor for both of these is identical, 0.142046. When this is multiplied by the face value of $1,000, the deposit required today is the answer:

$$0.142046 \times \$1,000 = \$142.05$$

If the effective interest rate is not available on a table, you will need to apply the present-value formula at the effective rate. The formula for the present value of a bond is summarized in Figure 10.1.

YIELD COMPARISONS

The value of a bond can be defined in several ways. The rating assigned to the bond (by Moody's or Standard & Poor's, for example) is a starting point for many investors, who seek safe investments and are willing to give up a portion of available yield, or who are willing to assume greater risks for higher returns.

Beyond the rating, however, bonds must be evaluated on the basis of maturity, coupon, and price. Those who purchase shares of bond mutual funds can evaluate the portfolio management's performance on the same basis.

The stated yield of a bond is not enough to make a comparison, unless all bonds are bought at par, and all have the same number of years until maturity. The nominal yield (or coupon rate) is only the starting point for the realistic analysis.

$$\frac{FV}{(1 + r)^t} = PV$$

FV = face value
r = rate per half-year
t = number of half-year periods
PV = present value

EXAMPLE: 20 YEARS, 10%:

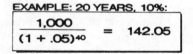

$$\frac{1,000}{(1 + .05)^{40}} = 142.05$$

FIGURE 10.1 Present value of a bond.

Example: A bond offers a coupon rate of 10 percent. The current yield on the same bond will be higher if the bond is purchased at a discount, or lower if the bond is purchased at a premium.

When the bond is at 100 (par), the current yield and the coupon rate are identical. The current market value of a bond may fall, when its interest rate is less attractive than those offered on other bonds. The current market value will rise when outside interest rates fall. Thus, the market value of bonds is a constantly changing factor.

To compute the current yield on a bond, divide the coupon amount by the current market price. Examples of this calculation are shown in Figure 10.2.

Current yield is a simple calculation. However, it does not accurately express yield in the event a bond is held until maturity, since the varying market price of the bond over time will affect total return. In order to accurately compare bonds, it will be necessary to calculate the yield to maturity.

YIELD TO MATURITY

This expression of yield is a dependable method for comparing bonds to one another, or for developing the equivalent yield on outside investments. Our purpose is not to evaluate the proper applications of yield to maturity,

$$\frac{C}{P} = Y$$

C = coupon amount
P = today's price
Y = current yield

DISCOUNT EXAMPLE

$$\frac{\$100}{\$960} = 10.42\%$$

PREMIUM EXAMPLE

$$\frac{\$80}{\$1,030} = 7.77\%$$

FIGURE 10.2 Formula: Current yield.

but to simplify the process so that it can be performed with minimal effort. Thus, the comparison of one bond to another will be as accurate as possible.

The best method for calculating yield to maturity involves spreading the discount or premium at the point of purchase, over the remaining term of the bond. But the purpose of the calculation is not to identify the exact yield; rather, we must develop the means for a fairly accurate comparison.

Yield to maturity involves calculating two separate yields, and then taking an average:

1. **Income to purchase price:** The first yield compares annual income to the actual purchase price of the bond. For the purposes of calculating yield to maturity, annual income is the coupon amount, adjusted by a yearly average amortization of discount or accrual of premium.
2. **Annual yield to par value:** The second part of yield to maturity involves comparing annual income (interest adjusted for discount or premium), as a percentage of par value adjusted for annual average discount or premium.

Example: The yield-to-maturity calculation is performed on a discount bond and on a premium bond, available at different times and under different market conditions. This enables the investor to calculate the effects of a changing interest market on long-term yields in a portfolio. The first is a 10% bond with five years until maturity, purchased at 96. Second is an 8% bond with four years until maturity, purchased at 103.

To calculate yield to maturity:

	DISCOUNT BOND	PREMIUM BOND
Yield A		
1. Enter par value	$ 1,000	$ 1,000
2. Subtract the purchase price to arrive at discount or premium amount	− 960	−1,030
	$ 40	$− 30
3. Enter years to maturity	5	4
4. Divide discount or premium by years to maturity to determine the annual average	$ 8	$ −7.50
5. Enter the annual coupon amount	100	80
6. Net the sums in steps 4 and 5 to determine annual net income	$ 108	$ 72.50

Yield A

	DISCOUNT BOND	PREMIUM BOND
7. Enter the purchase price	$ 960	$ 1,030
8. Divide annual net income (step 6) by purchase price (step 7) to determine Yield A	11.25%	7.04%

Yield B

	DISCOUNT BOND	PREMIUM BOND
1. Enter par value	$ 1,000	$ 1,000
2. Enter the average annual discount or premium (Yield A, step 4)	8	−7.50
3. Subtract the discount or add the premium in step 2 from par value to determine adjusted cost	$ 992	$ 1,007.50
4. Enter annual net income (Yield A computation, step 6)	108	72.50
5. Divide annual net income (step 4) by adjusted cost (step 3) to determine Yield B	10.89%	7.20%

Yield to Maturity

	DISCOUNT BOND	PREMIUM BOND
1. Enter Yield A	11.25%	7.04%
2. Enter Yield B	10.89%	7.20%
3. Add the two yields	22.14%	14.24%
4. Divide by 2 to arrive at Yield to Maturity	2	2
=	11.07%	7.12%

A worksheet that reduces this series of calculations down to a few steps is given in Figure 10.3.

A series of published Bond Yield Tables provide the actual yields to maturity, and are set up much like the interest calculation tables discussed in previous chapters. The tables provide the following:

1. Coupon rate;
2. Columns for years to maturity;

STEP 1	par value	$_____
STEP 2	less: purchase price	– $_____
STEP 3	equals: discount or premium	= $_____
STEP 4	years to maturity	_____
STEP 5	step 3 ÷ step 4	= $_____
STEP 6	annual coupon	+ $_____
STEP 7	step 5 + step 6	= $_____
STEP 8	purchase price	$_____
STEP 9	step 7 ÷ step 8	= _____ %
STEP 10	enter step 1	$_____
STEP 11	less: step 5	– $_____
STEP 12	equals: adjusted cost	= $_____
STEP 13	enter step 7	$_____
STEP 14	step 13 ÷ step 12	= _____ %
STEP 15	enter step 9	+ _____ %
STEP 16	step 14 + step 15	+ _____ %
STEP 17	step 16 ÷ 2	= _____ %

FIGURE 10.3   Worksheet: Yield to maturity.

3. Rows for purchase price or current value;
4. Yields.

The following tables show the actual yields to maturity for the two bonds used in the previous example. The 10 percent table reports that a bond purchased at 96 with five years until maturity yields 11.06; our calculation resulted in 11.07. The 8 percent table reports that a bond purchased at 103 with four years until maturity yields 7.12, the same as our calculation revealed.

The tables are useful for calculating yield to maturity when the percentages and prices listed conform to the actual values for a particular bond. However, chances are that the values with which you will deal in your own comparisons may fall between table values. Thus, being able to calculate the exact yield to maturity is a distinct advantage.

Bond Yield Table

10 PERCENT	Years to Maturity				
PRICE	3	4	5	6	7
95.00	12.03	11.60	11.34	11.17	11.04
95.50	11.83	11.43	11.20	11.05	10.94
96.00	11.62	11.27	11.06	10.93	10.83
96.50	11.41	11.11	10.93	10.81	10.72
97.00	11.20	10.95	10.79	10.69	10.62

Bond Yield Table

8 PERCENT	Years to Maturity				
PRICE	2	3	4	5	6
101.00	7.45	7.62	7.70	7.75	7.79
102.00	6.91	7.25	7.41	7.51	7.58
103.00	6.38	6.88	7.12	7.27	7.37
104.00	5.85	6.51	6.84	7.04	7.17
105.00	5.33	6.15	6.56	6.80	6.97

It takes less time to refer to a book of bond yield tables than to work through a calculation with 17 steps. However, just as compound interest tables will not always be available for the interest rates you seek, bond yield tables cannot possibly provide every fractional purchase price and interest rate you will use.

The yield to maturity calculation can be expressed in a single formula:

$$\frac{\dfrac{ANI}{P} + \dfrac{ANI}{M - APY}}{2},$$

where
$$ANI = \text{Annual net income,}$$
$$P = \text{Purchase Price,}$$
$$M = \text{Maturity,}$$
$$APY = \text{Average per year.}$$

However, to use this formula, it will first be necessary to calculate ANI and APY. Having to take these steps to make the singular formula work leads inevitably to the methodical, multiple-step process shown in Figure 10.4.

The reason for breaking the calculation into five steps will become apparent to anyone who attempts a single calculation. The five breakdowns isolate key values that are necessary for subsequent steps in the calculation.

These five formulas can be labeled, based on the information they provide:

1. Average per year (discount);
2. Annual net income;
3. Yield A;
4. Yield B;
5. Yield to maturity.

Application of the formula to calculate yield to maturity for a discounted bond is shown in Figure 10.5, and for a premium bond in Figure 10.6.

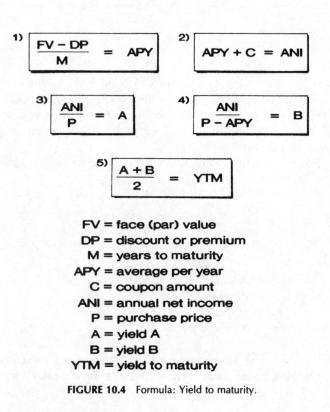

1) $$\frac{FV - DP}{M} = APY$$

2) $$APY + C = ANI$$

3) $$\frac{ANI}{P} = A$$

4) $$\frac{ANI}{P - APY} = B$$

5) $$\frac{A + B}{2} = YTM$$

FV = face (par) value
DP = discount or premium
M = years to maturity
APY = average per year
C = coupon amount
ANI = annual net income
P = purchase price
A = yield A
B = yield B
YTM = yield to maturity

FIGURE 10.4   Formula: Yield to maturity.

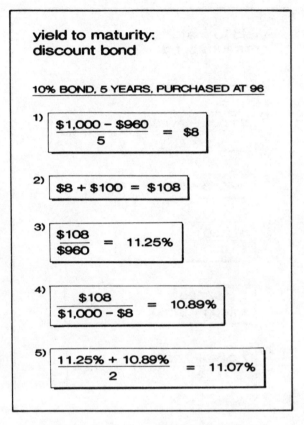

FIGURE 10.5   Yield to maturity: Discount bond.

INTERPOLATION

The various calculations of yield and current market value can be achieved by interpolation. For example, when a bond's coupon rate is 10.25 percent, and the available yield to maturity tables list only 10 and 10.5, the approximate yield can be calculated by averaging the rates above and below.

Example: A bond is currently priced at 98, and will mature in 13 years. Its coupon rate is 10.25 percent. Your book of bond yield tables reports yields at 10 percent and 10.5 percent only:

Percent	Y.T.M.
10	10.28%
10.5	10.79%

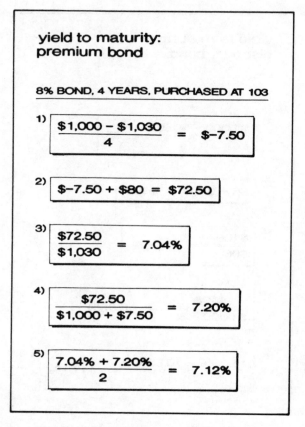

FIGURE 10.6 Yield to maturity: Premium bond.

To interpolate the yield to maturity at 10.25, add the two table yields together, and divide by two:

$$\frac{10.28 + 10.79}{2} = 10.54\%.$$

This total agrees with the table yield to maturity for 10.25 percent. To calculate the yield to maturity for fractional units not exactly halfway between those available, carry the interpolation a step farther.

With the knowledge that the yield to maturity is 10.28 percent (10 percent coupon rate), and 10.54 percent (interpolated rate for 10.25 percent), what is the yield to maturity for a bond with a coupon rate of 10.125 percent?

Interpolation:

$$\frac{10.28 + 10.54}{2} = 10.41\%.$$

The same rules of interpolation can be applied vertically. For example, you want to estimate the yield to maturity for a 10 percent bond with a price of 95.75, but the bond yield tables show yields only for 95.50 and 96.00. The maturity is three years. The table reports:

Price	Y.T.M.
95.50	11.83%
96.00	11.62%

To interpolate:

$$\frac{11.83 + 11.62}{2} = 11.73.$$

The actual yield to maturity is 11.72, so our calculation is off by one one-hundredth of a percent due to rounding.

Interpolation can also be applied to calculations of present value, as used to figure out the current market value of a bond. A reasonable estimate of present value will prove adequate, when interpolation is an alternative to executing 40 or 50 calculations. This will become an issue when the interest rate is not available on tables, and the present value of 1 per period (for coupon payment values) must be computed. In this instance, use table rates above and below the coupon rate, and interpolate the average.

Many investment decisions are made on the basis of historical performance, such as the decision to purchase shares of one mutual fund over another, or to buy stock directly. However, bond analysis is concerned with the future, since it can be known and calculated precisely.

11

Math for Mutual Funds

Mutual funds allow investors to diversify over a broad range of investments, and also to select a specific risk level in line with personal criteria. However, while funds manage a pooled investment portfolio, the selection is not always a straightforward one. Confusion over the real level of fees and expenses, computation of return on investment, and analysis of a fund's management make the selection of a mutual fund more complex than it appears at first glance.

However, the problems of identifying a consistent standard for comparison are overcome by applying certain tests for value and profit, based both on historical information (for trend analysis) and on the current status of a fund (in terms of cash availability, level of net asset value, and net income).

The evaluation of value and profits in mutual funds can apply in three ways:

1. To an individual's portfolio;
2. To a single fund's performance;
3. To the mutual fund market as a whole, or in comparing mutual fund status to overall market trends.

Of greatest interest to most investors is the first category. Specific mathematical tests will reveal the value of an account, and the annualized returns that have been earned over time. A mutual fund investment cannot be made and forgotten, a belief held by many investors. The quality of professional management varies between funds, and can change over time, the mix of its portfolio, and performance in changing market conditions.

The second category includes analysis of a single fund's performance in the past, reflected in current net asset, net income, and expense ratios.

In addition, investors must carefully compare the fees and costs involved with each fund, to determine the net amount that will be retained after making the decision to invest.

Fund performance can be evaluated in the context of fundamental or technical indicators, or with a combination of both. Or overall fund status can be used as an indicator itself. Institutional investing, especially the activity of mutual funds, represents a large portion of total market action, so fund indicators are given a great deal of weight by many analysts.

In this chapter, we will explain the measurements of mutual fund values and profits, and show how fund indicators are used to determine investment profitability.

COMPARING FEES

Due to the complexity and scope of other fees and expenses, a simple comparison between two or more mutual fund investments is not possible on the single basis of whether or not a sales load is charged. The decision to buy load or no-load fund shares is only a superficial means for making a decision. A no-load fund is not always less expensive than a load fund. The level of management fees and other costs and expenses must be included in the equation.

> *Example:* You plan to invest $2,000 in a mutual fund account, and expect it to grow at the compounded rate of 15 percent per year. In determining which fund to select, you include both load and no-load funds. One fund you evaluate charges a sales load of 8 percent, and assesses management fees and expenses of 1 percent of net assets per year. A second has no load, but charges expenses equal to 2 percent of net assets per year.

A comparison between these two funds, assuming both earn 15 percent per year, reveals the true cost over time. The annual "net" yield equals the assumed 15 percent return, less annual expense levels. Thus, the load fund's net earnings will equal 14 percent (15 percent assumed annual earnings rate, less 1 percent expense fee); and the no-load fund's net earnings will equal 13 percent (15 percent assumed annual earnings rate, less 2 percent expense fee):

When a load fund's expense level is lower than a comparable no-load fund, the load fund will ultimately prove to be less expensive. That's because the load is charged only once, at the point at which the investment is made. However, the expense fee is assessed each and every year. For the purpose of example, we will demonstrate how an investment in a load fund is less expensive if the account remains open for ten years or more:

	LOAD	NO-LOAD
Initial Investment	$2,000	$2,000
Less: Sales Load, 8%	− 160	
Net Initial Value	$1,840	$2,000
Year 1 Net Yield	258	260
Ending Value	$2,098	$2,260
Year 2 Net Yield	294	294
Ending Value	$2,392	$2,554
Year 3 Net Yield	335	332
Ending Value	$2,727	$2,886
Year 4 Net Yield	382	375
Ending Value	$3,109	$3,261
Year 5 Net Yield	435	424
Ending Value	$3,544	$3,685
Year 6 Net Yield	496	479
Ending Value	$4,040	$4,164
Year 7 Net Yield	566	541
Ending Value	$4,606	$4,705
Year 8 Net Yield	645	612
Ending Value	$5,251	$5,317
Year 9 Net Yield	735	691
Ending Value	$5,986	$6,008
Year 10 Net Yield	838	781
Ending Value	$6,824	$6,789

This ten-year analysis reveals that, given the assumptions about equal investment potential, the load fund is ultimately more profitable. Because the expense element repeats each year, long-term mutual fund investors cannot limit their analysis strictly to the comparison of initial loading. The mathematical models you build to select the best possible investment must carry through to the full length of the holding period you anticipate.

Example: You compare two funds you believe to have equal potential for earnings. However, one, a load fund, charges a lower expense fee than the no-load fund. The decision to purchase shares in one fund or the other must be based on a comparison between two factors:

1. The length of time that will be required for the no-load fund to become more profitable.

2. The holding period you anticipate.

In our example above, an investor who planned to close an account before the tenth year would realize a greater profit by purchasing the no-load fund. However, if the account remained open for 10 years or more, the load fund would represent a better buy.

This conclusion assumes that earnings in each fund will be comparable, and that the current expense levels of each will remain constant. These are uncertainties, because funds change policies, and expense levels change over time. Investors can make final decisions based only on information that is available at the moment, and cannot possibly estimate future changes in expense levels, profits, or market performance.

The analysis of fees must also include back-end load, exit fees, and 12b-1 fees:

Back-end load is also called a contingent deferred sales charge. It is assessed in the event that assets are withdrawn before a stated period of time has expired. For example, one fund charges a fee that is equal to 6 percent of an account's value, on any withdrawals taking place by the end of the first year. This charge decreases by 1 percent per year; so if no withdrawals occur by the end of the sixth year, there will be no back-end load. In comparing funds, if you anticipate closing an account prior to the expiration of the back-end load period, you must include an estimate of the fee in the comparison.

Exit fees, or **redemption fees**, are charged by only a handful of funds. Up to 1 percent of the account's value is deducted upon withdrawal when exit fees apply. The fee may also be stated as a flat dollar amount. In some cases, the fee applies to withdrawals taken during a stated period of time; in others, the fee applies indefinitely. Like the back-end load, any applicable exit fees must be included in a comparative calculation of future profitability.

12b-1 fees are fees that mutual funds may assess for the cost of advertising or, in some cases, to compensate brokers in lieu of commissions. The name comes from the Securities and Exchange Commission ruling in 1980 that allowed inclusion of this fee for the first time. This fee, averaging 1 to 1.25 percent of assets per year, may be included in the total of expenses reported in a fund's prospectus, or it may be included separately. In order to make your comparison valid, you will first need to determine (a) whether or not a 12b-1 fee is assessed, and (b) whether the fee is reported as part of annual expenses, or as a separate number. It is possible that a mutual fund you select today will not charge a 12b-1 fee, but may institute it in the future. Thus, a decision based on the current absence of this fee could prove flawed—especially when the fee changes the estimate of profitability and makes another fund the more viable choice.

COMPUTING ANNUALIZED RETURN

The preliminary decision to invest in one fund or another must be made with complete recognition of the effect that various fees and costs will have each year. The sales load applies each time a deposit is made, while 12b-1 fees and expenses are deducted from the total value of your account, and recur on an annual basis.

Figuring out the rate of return on a mutual fund investment is simple—as long as a single deposit is made, no redemptions occur, and all dividends and capital gains are reinvested. However, many investors deposit money each month, take some initial capital out, elect to receive dividends and capital gains in cash, or may alter the terms in effect when the account is first opened. Any of these circumstances makes the computation more complex.

In any computation of return, when you have changed the terms of your account, it might be necessary to go through two separate calculations.

Example: For the first three years that you own shares in a mutual fund, you elect to receive dividends and capital gains in cash. During that same period, you make one initial deposit of $1,000 and subsequently pay in $200 per quarter. At the beginning of the fourth year, you change your election and instruct the fund to reinvest all dividends and capital gains; you also begin depositing $100 per month.

To compute the average annual rate of return in these circumstances, the clearest method will be first to compute the three-year average, and then to compute the return from the fourth year forward, using the fund's value (adjusted for withdrawals and cash payments) as of the end of the third year. The rates of return for each separated period should then be weighted, and an annual average rate calculated.

To compute a weighted rate of return, use the number of months in each period as a numerator, and the total months in the entire holding period as a denominator.

Example: You have had money invested in a mutual account for the last 60 months. During the first 36 months, you took dividends and capital gains in cash. During the last 24 months, you reinvested all earnings, and also changed the frequency of deposits. You calculate the rate of return for each period separately, and conclude the following:

Net Profit, months 1 to 36   = 17.45%
Net Profit, months 37 to 60 = 22.60%

A weighted average must account for the fact that the earlier period is longer than the later one. Thus, the calculation for the average over 60 months is:

a) $$\frac{36}{60} \times 17.45\% = 10.47;$$

b) $$\frac{24}{60} \times 22.60\% = 9.04;$$

c) $$10.47 + 9.04 = 19.51\%.$$

The formula for weighted return is shown in Figure 11.1.

The calculation of the annualized rate of return must be based not only on the increased value of your account, but also with allowance for changes during the holding period. Thus, if you redeem a portion of your portfolio, or if you make subsequent deposits, then the *average* capital available to you during the holding period must be modified. Otherwise, the calculation will be inaccurate.

The same adjustment must be made if you elected to receive dividends and capital gains in cash, rather than reinvesting income. In that case, the current value of your account must be increased for the amount you received from the fund.

Example: You want to compute the annualized rate of return for a mutual fund investment you made six months ago. You originally deposited $5,000, but later withdrew $1,000. You also received $50 in cash for dividends and capital gains paid by the fund. The

$$\left(\frac{M1}{T} \times r \right) + \left(\frac{M2}{T} \times r \right) = W$$

M1 = months in first period
M2 = months in second period
T = total holding period
r = rate of return
W = weighted return

$$\left(\frac{36}{60} \times 17.45\% \right) + \left(\frac{24}{60} \times 22.60\% \right) = 19.51\%$$

FIGURE 11.1 Weighted return.

reported value of the account is now $7,000. To compute the annualized rate of return:

Step 1:	Enter the Current Value of the Account	$7,000
Step 2:	Enter the Amount of Distributions Received	$ 50
Step 3:	Enter the Amount of Redemptions	$1,000
Step 4:	Divide the Redemption Total by 2	$ 500
Step 5:	Enter the Initial Investment Amount	$5,000
Step 6:	Add Steps 4 and 5 to Determine Average Basis	$5,500
Step 7:	Step 1 + Step 2 − Step 4	$6,550
Step 8:	Divide Step 7 by Step 6	1.1909
Step 9:	Compute the Percent of Profit:	

$$(\text{Step } 8 - 1) \times 100 = \quad 19.09\%$$

Step 10:	Enter Months Held	6
Step 11:	Annualize the Return:	

$$\frac{\text{Step } 10}{12} \times \text{Step } 9 = \quad 9.545\%$$

This computation can be completed using the worksheet in Figure 11.2.

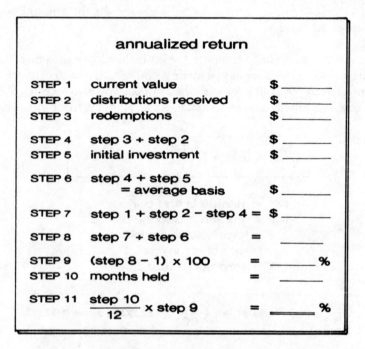

FIGURE 11.2 Annualized return.

The average basis must include an allowance for any redemptions taken during the holding period of the fund, because the available capital was not the same at the beginning of each month. The same argument applies when a fund is established, and a series of subsequent deposits is made.

Example: You started your mutual fund investment program one year ago by depositing $2,000. Since then, you have deposited $200 per month:

Initial Deposit	$2,000
11 months, $200 per month	2,200
Total Basis	$4,200

This total cannot be used to compute annualized return, since the account's basis (initial investment) changes each month. To figure out the average basis, the time value of each deposit in the series must be expressed as a fraction of the total.

In this example, the initial deposit was made 12 months ago. Thus, on an annualized basis, it is worth 12/12, or full value. However, each subsequent deposit must be adjusted fractionally to reflect initial investment on the same 12-month basis. On a chart, this would require a series of computations for each deposit:

MONTH	FACTOR		DEPOSIT		ADJUSTED VALUE
Jan	12/12	×	$2,000	=	$2,000
Feb	11/12	×	200	=	183
Mar	10/12	×	200	=	167
Apr	9/12	×	200	=	150
May	8/12	×	200	=	133
Jun	7/12	×	200	=	117
Jul	6/12	×	200	=	100
Aug	5/12	×	200	=	83
Sep	4/12	×	200	=	67
Oct	3/12	×	200	=	50
Nov	2/12	×	200	=	33
Dec	1/12	×	200	=	17
			Average Basis		$3,100

This is not a complicated process, assuming that the period of analysis is short, and the amount of monthly deposit does not change. However, it can be computed with only two steps, rather than 12. The total of the months' values shown in the table above, divided by 12, gives the single fraction required to compute the average basis for months 2 through 11:

$$1 + 2 + 3 + 4 + 5 + 6 + 7 + 8 + 9 + 10 + 11 = 66.$$

Thus, when the total of months held is divided by the value of a full year, the average initial investment is the result:

$$\$200 \times \frac{66}{12} = \$1,100.$$

This, added to the first month's value, results in the same total as monthly computations produce:

$$\$1,100 + \$2,000 = \$3,100.$$

One way of expressing the average basis is to describe it as the amount of capital available for the full year. Thus, when $200 is deposited at the beginning of the fifth month, only 8/12 of that, or $133, is available to earn money for the average annualized period.

The formula for average basis is shown in Figure 11.3.

This computation is especially practical when you are trying to figure out the average annualized basis over the course of a year, but when the amount of monthly deposit has been altered during the period.

1)
$$D \times \frac{M}{12} = A$$

2)
$$A + \ldots A = B$$

D = amount deposited
M = months held
A = average initial value
B = average basis

1)
$$2,000 \times \frac{12}{12} = 2,000$$

$$200 \times \frac{66}{12} = 1,100$$

2)
$$2,000 + 1,100 = 3,100$$

FIGURE 11.3   Average basis.

Example: You started your mutual fund investment program one year ago, when you deposited $2,000. Over the remaining 11 months, you made the following subsequent deposits:

Months 2 through 5	$100 per month
Months 6 through 8	$200 per month
Months 9 through 11	$350 per month
Month 12	$150 per month

To compute the average basis for this entire period, the formula is applied to each segment of deposits:

MONTH	AMOUNT	AVAILABLE
2	$100	11
3	100	10
4	100	9
5	100	8
6	200	7
7	200	6
8	200	5
9	350	4
10	350	3
11	350	2
12	150	1

Next, the segments are broken down into their appropriate multipliers:

$100 per month:
11 + 10 + 9 + 8 = 38.
$200 per month:
7 + 6 + 5 = 18.
$350 per month:
4 + 3 + 2 = 9.
$150 per month:
1

Since months 2 through 11 must equal a total numerator of 66, we can verify that the totals above are correct:

38 + 18 + 9 + 1 = 66.

Next, the four segments representing months 2 through 11 are multiplied, and added to the full-year value of the initial deposit:

a) $$\frac{38}{12} \times \$100 = \$317;$$

b) $$\frac{18}{12} \times \$200 = \$300;$$

c) $$\frac{9}{12} \times \$350 = \$263;$$

d) $$\frac{1}{12} \times \$150 = \$12.$$

The initial deposit of $2,000 is counted at full value, since it was available for 12/12 of the year. The total adjusted basis in this example is:

$$\$317 + \$300 + \$263 + \$12 + \$2,000 = \$2,892.$$

To prove the calculation:

MONTH	FACTOR		DEPOSIT		ADJUSTED VALUE
Jan	12/12	×	$2,000	=	$2,000
Feb	11/12	×	100	=	92
Mar	10/12	×	100	=	83
Apr	9/12	×	100	=	75
May	8/12	×	100	=	67
Jun	7/12	×	200	=	117
Jul	6/12	×	200	=	100
Aug	5/12	×	200	=	83
Sep	4/12	×	350	=	117
Oct	3/12	×	350	=	88
Nov	2/12	×	350	=	58
Dec	1/12	×	150	=	12
			Average Basis		$2,892

The same computations can be performed on holdings for periods greater than one year. However, in that case, the denominator of the fraction must be adjusted to reflect the longer period of months, and the final percentage of return must then be divided by the number of years, to arrive at the average annual return.

EVALUATING A FUND

In the preceding section, calculations described the annualized rate of return on an investment, based on the average availability of capital during a holding period. A second level of analysis is concerned with the performance of a specific mutual fund, for the purpose of determining:

1. Buy, hold, or sell signals;
2. Changes in trends;
3. Performance in comparison to the market.

A common method of selecting funds is to review past experience. However, the expectation that a specific mutual fund's management will be able to repeat a past earnings record is questionable. Whenever the future is judged based solely on historical information, you must expect the analysis to be uncertain.

The testing of a fund's asset and earning strength, especially when analyzed as part of a trend, is more indicative of management's ability to produce consistent results. This may translate to better than average growth during bull markets, and to less than average declines during bear markets.

The most commonly applied test is net asset value (NAV), which is the mutual fund's equivalent of share price; NAV is computed by adding the current market value of the fund's invested portfolio, to the total of cash on hand, and then dividing that total by the number of shares outstanding. The market value of invested assets in this calculation is net of the fund's liabilities. The formula for NAV is shown in Figure 11.4.

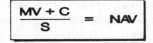

$$\frac{MV + C}{S} = NAV$$

MV = market value of invested assets
C = cash on hand
S = number of shares outstanding
NAV = net asset value

$$\frac{\$325.1 + \$1.2\ \text{million}}{24,135,000} = \$13.52$$

FIGURE 11.4 Net asset value.

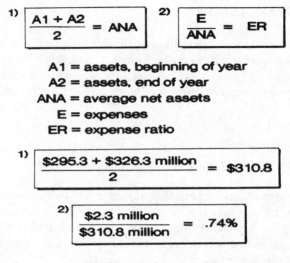

FIGURE 11.5   Expense ratio.

Net asset value serves as a useful test of a fund management's ability to produce consistent profits. This is most applicable when an open-end fund is experiencing a substantial growth pattern. As the number of shares outstanding increases, and as the size of the invested portfolio grows, the ability to alter the portfolio may change as well. A deterioration in the fund's market value per share will be reflected in a changing NAV. Or a well-managed fund may be able to offset the change with a decreasing trend level in expenses charged against assets. In either case, NAV provides an important test of market value, as part of a trend.

Your personal rate of return, computed on an annualized basis, must take into consideration the redemption of initial capital, subsequent deposits, and dividends or capital gains received in cash. However, the fund itself reports a net income ratio based on annual performance. This net income ratio is figured by dividing net income by average assets.

A third test of mutual fund performance, especially useful for comparing the cost of investing between two or more funds, is the expense ratio. This reveals the annual expense deducted from total assets. It is computed by dividing total expenses charged, by average net assets of the fund. The formula is shown in Figure 11.5.

FUNDS AND TECHNICAL ANALYSIS

Beyond analysis of an individual portfolio or one fund's historical performance, mutual fund trends may provide important technical indicators, to

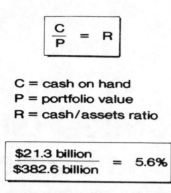

FIGURE 11.6   Cash-to-assets ratio.

anticipate market highs and lows or to signal impending changes in direction. Funds represent a significant portion of the total market, and many contrarians believe that fund management is usually wrong in its judgment of market conditions.

With that belief in mind, the contrarian assumes that when fund management is generally cautious, meaning a high level of cash is being held in reserve, that will signal a market bottom. And when fund management is extremely optimistic, reflected in a nearly fully invested cash position, that is taken as a signal that the market is at or near a top.

The cash-to-assets ratio, also known as the fund liquidity ratio, is a comparison between cash on hand and the total portfolio value. A historical review of this trend shows that a growing ratio level (increased cash) occurs at market bottoms, and minimal reserves are found near or at market tops. However, applying this information to the current market will prove less exact than historical review.

The ratio is computed on a monthly basis, using information for a broad range of funds. It is then charted as part of a 12-month moving average. The amount of cash on hand for the funds in the range is divided by the current value of portfolios owned by the funds. The formula is summarized in Figure 11.6.

The analysis of a mutual fund account, a specific fund, or the effects of mutual funds on the overall market require careful and concise calculation, including modifications of basis with changing investment levels during the holding period. The need for careful definition and a variety of different calculations also applies to real estate investing. This is the topic of the next chapter.

12

Math for Real Estate Investments

The historically sound growth and safety of real estate has made this one of the most successful forms of investment. Individuals can purchase residential property to live in or to rent; units of limited partnerships; or shares of real estate investment trusts.

Each method for purchasing real estate must be evaluated and compared on the basis of structure and risk features. In this chapter, we will explain five areas of math for the real estate market:

1. Computations of basis, cash flow, profits, and rates of return.
2. Financial calculations.
3. Rental income property.
4. Appraisal math.
5. Measurements of land and structures.

A fair comparison between two or more real estate investments cannot necessarily be made on a like basis. In addition to allowing for the cost and potential return from placing money directly or through a pool, you must also keep three major risk factors in mind.

RISK FACTORS IN REAL ESTATE

The three factors to remember concerning risk are:

1. Diversification: Is your portfolio fairly diversified after investing in real estate? If you will be required to make a down payment, and also to assume a liability for many years of mortgage payments, how does that affect your diversification standards?

The second issue involves the degree of diversification within a pooled investment. For example, you purchase units of a real estate limited partnership. How well diversified is the partnership itself? Is it diversified in terms of the type of property it holds, the tenants it enters lease contracts with, and the region of the country?

2. Liquidity: Most forms of real estate investment are illiquid. Funds must be left invested over many years, or can be withdrawn only by taking a loss. One important exception is the real estate investment trust (REIT). Shares of trusts are traded on the public exchanges, just like common stock. At the same time, the funds are diversified within the trust.

Some methods for investing in real estate involve an illiquid market as well. For example, the limited partnership form lacks a secondary market, so that it might be difficult or impossible to sell units once they are purchased.

3. Leverage: How leveraged is your real estate investment, and what does that mean in terms of net income? Some partnerships, for example, may employ high leverage to purchase a number of properties; other pools may involve all-cash deals, with no borrowings. The latter will present a lower risk, since the program could afford higher vacancy rates without suffering a negative cash flow.

Leverage is not always a negative factor in selecting a real estate investment. Most homeowners leverage up to 80 percent of their purchase price, and reduce the debt over as long as 30 years.

The point about leverage is that when interest payments must be made, the real net profit is drastically reduced. Property values must grow at a rate above the overall payment to a lender, if the investor is to earn any real after-tax profits. The deductibility of interest should not be an issue to argue against this point. Even after allowing for the tax benefits of deducting interest expenses, the profit and cash flow question remains a crucial one for comparing different real estate investments.

With these three risk factors in the real estate equation, it is not possible to compare two unlike investments on a fair basis. For example, will you do better investing in your own home, or in shares of a real estate investment trust?

The answer must be based on assumptions about future property values, growth rates in the region where the property is located, and—most of all—by the factors of diversification, liquidity, and leverage. An investment that appears to offer better potential for growth may be less desirable because the risk factors do not suit your personal standards or limits. Another consideration is the intended use. A residence you plan to live in is not primarily an investment, but a personal asset. If and when you sell, you will certainly increase your net worth if property values have risen and your equity has been increased by loan payments. However, the purpose of buying a residence must be different from the purpose of investing in a pooled program, or for buying a home you plan to rent out to someone else.

Complicating the question of comparisons even more, real estate values vary by regions. In the selection of one investment over another, you cannot depend on national averages to determine whether apartments or warehouse space represent the more promising way to go. So when you compare a program that owns office space in Houston, to one that has cooperative units in New York City, it is important to acknowledge that the two markets are vastly different. This difference relates to growth potential, current and future supply and demand, regional competition for mortgage loans, population trends, and current value. So comparing unlike programs against identical criteria is not realistic.

TERMINOLOGY

The definitions involved with real estate returns, yields, and basis can confuse investors. In order to ensure that your comparisons are made on a like basis, it is first necessary to distinguish the words and phrases that will come up, both in historical reports and in projections of future performance.

The basis is the original cost of real estate. However, that word, by itself, does not explain precisely what number is being used. For this reason, the term *adjusted basis* has developed. This is the purchase price, plus closing costs paid, plus the cost of improvements, and minus any depreciation claimed.

Adjusted basis has special significance for computing and adjusting the profit from sale of property, for income tax purposes. It also is applied in various calculations of yield from real estate investments.

Adjusted Basis	
Purchase price	$115,000
Plus: Closing costs	2,500
Plus: Cost of improvements	22,000
Sub-total	$139,500
Less: Depreciation	11,000
Adjusted Basis	$128,500

The sales price must also be adjusted to allow for closing costs and real estate commissions paid. In cases where property is renovated in anticipation of a sale, the fixing-up expenses must be deducted from the sales price, in addition to the costs of sale, to arrive at the true, adjusted sales price:

Adjusted Sales Price	
Contract price	$164,000
Less: Closing costs	− 11,200
Less: Fixing-up expenses	− 4,000
Adjusted Sales Price	$148,800

With both purchase and sales prices adjusted for all costs involved, the true net profit can be computed:

Adjusted sales price	$148,800
Less: Adjusted purchase price	128,500
Net Profit	$ 20,300

These calculations can be applied to either residential or income property. In cases of income property alone, two additional tests are applied.

The first of these is a calculation of total return, over a period of years. As with all forms of investment, the precise definition of yield depends on the source. This is one reason that great care and caution must be taken whenever you compare projections, or even historical information reported in a program's prospectus. Be sure that the "yield" being reported by each program is identical, or your comparison will be misleading.

A fairly simple calculation of total return reduces the percentage return to a yearly average:

Total Return	
Adjusted sales price	$148,800
Less: Adjusted purchase price	128,500
Capital Gain	$ 20,300
Plus: Net rental income	37,300
Plus: Tax benefits	2,400
Total Profit	$ 60,000
Total Return (Total profit divided by purchase price)	46.7%
Years owned	7.5
Average Annual Total Return (Total return divided by years owned)	6.23%

The second rental income calculation is for after-tax cash flow. The importance of this as a means for comparisons between two dissimilar programs is that it enables you to deduct the financial consequences of taxation from cash flow (or, in some cases, to add tax benefits).

Cash flow must be computed for real estate comparisons, because operating profit is meaningless by itself. The investor must also ensure that available, after-tax cash flow is adequate for the required debt service on the mortgage loan.

The computation follows:

After-tax Cash Flow	
Rent income	$24,000
Less: Operating expenses	− 8,300
Less: Mortgage interest	− 10,550
Taxable Income	$ 5,150
Less: Taxes	− 1,442
After-tax Income	$ 3,708
Less: Mortgage Principal	− 4,240
Plus: Depreciation	+ 4,000
After-tax Cash Flow	$ 3,468

Operating expenses in this example include depreciation, thus reducing taxable income. However, depreciation is not a cash expense; thus, it must be added back in after taxes have been computed. Mortgage principal is not deductible for tax purposes; however, it represents a cash payment, and must be deducted from the available cash flow.

RATES OF RETURN

Our first premise for computing return must be that simple program-to-program comparison is not always possible, nor is it accurate. Identical properties in identical regional economies can be evaluated on the same basis; but in most investment decisions, you are more likely to be faced with a review of dissimilar properties and regions.

For this reason, any comparison must be made first on the basis of potential income and then must be modified by the assumed future trends of supply and demand, risk characteristics, market value, and program features (all-cash, leverage, type of property, etc.).

All forms of real estate investment must be concerned with cash flow—the amount of money actually realized from the investment. In a highly leveraged program, this is the point of greatest risk. A reduction in vacancies could mean that the monthly mortgage payment cannot be met by current income. The calculation for cash-on-cash return compares cash flow to the original amount invested. This is demonstrated in Figure 12.1.

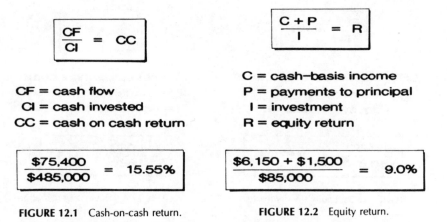

$$\frac{CF}{CI} = CC$$

CF = cash flow
CI = cash invested
CC = cash on cash return

$$\frac{C + P}{I} = R$$

C = cash–basis income
P = payments to principal
I = investment
R = equity return

$$\frac{\$75,400}{\$485,000} = 15.55\%$$

$$\frac{\$6,150 + \$1,500}{\$85,000} = 9.0\%$$

FIGURE 12.1   Cash-on-cash return.   FIGURE 12.2   Equity return.

This form of return is most useful to real estate investors as part of a trend. If cash flow—and the rate of return—decline due to a growing vacancy rate, then the market value of income property will fall as well. And when the cash-on-cash return grows each year, as the result of increasing rents and consistent control over vacancy levels, it indicates increasing property value.

A second version of cash flow calculation is the equity return. This formula allows for the benefits of cash flow, and adds the ever-increasing build-up of principal through mortgage payments. Thus, the "return" from a rental property is assumed to represent the sum of cash flow plus increases to principal. The formula is shown in Figure 12.2.

It is important to note that this calculation should involve the yearly *increases* to principal, and not the accumulated principal payments to date (which would include the original down payment, plus the cost of improvements). This is a yearly comparison, and should be viewed as part of a year-to-year trend.

A third version of return based on cash flow is the equity dividend rate. This calculation is performed on a pre-tax basis. Cash flow before tax consequences (or benefits) is divided by the amount of the original investment, as shown in Figure 12.3.

This formula enables the investor to track returns over a period of years, without the ever-changing effect of tax rates. A net, after-tax cash flow calculation will be changed when an individual's total taxable income rises or falls; or when tax brackets and rules for deducting expenses or limiting certain types of losses are changed as part of tax reform. These factors will distort the true economic picture of the real estate investment within the desired trend. Thus, a pre-tax calculation allows for greater accuracy in the comparison.

$$\boxed{\dfrac{CF}{I} = R}$$

CF = cash flow before taxes
I = investment
R = equity dividend rate

$$\boxed{\dfrac{\$3,950}{\$40,000} = 9.875\%}$$

FIGURE 12.3 Equity dividend rate.

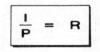

$$\boxed{\dfrac{I}{P} = R}$$

I = net operating income
P = annual loan payments
R = debt coverage ratio

$$\boxed{\dfrac{\$14,050}{\$12,680} = 1.11}$$

FIGURE 12.4 Debt coverage ratio.

FINANCIAL TESTS

In addition to determining whether a real estate investment is profitable (as defined by a cash flow calculation), investors must also be concerned with the status of their financing. Most real estate investors leverage their purchase through mortgage loans. The exception to this is the all-cash, unleveraged program.

The first test is called the debt coverage ratio. This compares net operating income to the annual total of loan payments. The purpose of this ratio is to show how income keeps pace with—or exceeds—the fixed repayment schedule. In the case of variable rate loans, this ratio also shows the effects of an increased annual debt service when net income is relatively stable. The formula is shown in Figure 12.4.

For the purpose of this ratio, "net operating income" refers to income less cash expenses, but excluding mortgage interest and principal. This is a modification from previous references to "net income," which did include interest expenses.

Another way that investors must analyze the financial aspects of a real estate investment is through comparison of the cost of financing. This is especially the case when a buyer is considering assuming an existing loan. Two similar properties could vary in desirability based solely on the rate of existing, assumable financing.

When two or more loans on a single property are outstanding, investors must calculate the average interest rate. This is a variation of computing the weighted average, as explained in a previous chapter.

Example: You are considering making an offer on an income property. Two existing loans are assumable. One is a 12.5 percent loan with a balance of $90,000, and the other is a 7.25 percent loan with

$$\left(\frac{P1}{P1 + P2} \times R1 \right) + \left(\frac{P2}{P1 + P2} \times R2 \right) = A$$

P1 = principal balance, loan 1
P2 = principal balance, loan 2
R1 = interest rate, loan 1
R2 = interest rate, loan 2
A = average rate

$$\left(\frac{90,000}{122,000} \times 12.5\% \right) + \left(\frac{32,000}{122,000} \times 7.25\% \right) = 11.12\%$$

FIGURE 12.5 Average interest rate.

a $32,000 balance. To calculate the average rate on this debt, the proportional mortgage balances must be divided by the total debt, and each side multiplied by the effective rate. This is shown in Figure 12.5.

A third financing test is the loan-to-balance ratio. This ratio may be used in one of two ways. First, a lender may establish limits on the amount that will be loaned on any one property. For example, one lender limits mortgage amounts with a loan-to-balance ratio of 80 percent (the lender will lend up to 80 percent of the appraised value).

Second, the calculation can be applied to estimate an owner's equity. For example, a property's current loan balance is $110,000, and the property is appraised at $137,500. The loan-to-balance ratio is 80 percent, as shown in Figure 12.6.

$$\frac{B}{A} = R$$

B = loan balance
A = appraised value
R = loan to balance ratio

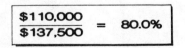

$$\frac{\$110,000}{\$137,500} = 80.0\%$$

FIGURE 12.6 Loan-to-balance ratio.

The mortgage constant is another formula that defines the status of debt on real estate. The amount of annual payments is divided by the original loan amount to determine the percentage. Given a particular rate of interest, time allowed for amortization, and the amount of the loan, the mortgage constant remains unchanged. In a variable rate loan, the mortgage constant is adjusted each time the rate increases or decreases.

Example: With a loan for $80,000 at 12 percent, and with a 30-year repayment schedule, your annual payments equal $9,874.80. This produces a mortgage constant of 12.3 percent. This formula is shown in Figure 12.7.

Property owners who contract for a fixed mortgage rate may find that refinancing will produce a profit, in the form of lower interest expenses. However, in order to refinance, a lender will charge points, closing costs, and in some instances, a prepayment penalty.

In order to decide whether refinancing is worth the expense involved, the owner must determine the time that will be required to absorb those costs, through reduced monthly expenses. This refinancing absorption rate is illustrated in Figure 12.8.

In the example shown, the total cost of refinancing a loan equals $3,725, and a reduced interest rate lowers the monthly payment by $148. Thus, it will take 25.2 months (just over two years) to break even, or to absorb the refinancing costs.

An investor faced with the refinancing question must determine whether the monthly savings justify the added cost, based on how long he or she plans to keep the investment. If plans call for a sale within the coming year, a two-year absorption rate will not be justified. However, if the investor plans to keep the property for well beyond the absorption period, refinancing will be a profitable change in the structure of financing. Once

$$\frac{P}{L} = C \qquad\qquad \frac{C}{S} = R$$

P = annual payments   C = cost of refinancing
L = original loan amount   S = savings per month
C = mortgage constant   R = absorption

$$\frac{\$9{,}874.80}{\$80{,}000} = 12.3\%$$

$$\frac{\$3{,}725}{\$148} = 25.2 \text{ months}$$

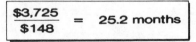

FIGURE 12.7 Mortgage constant.   **FIGURE 12.8** Refinancing absorption.

the breakeven point is exceeded, the investor's monthly expenses will be lower for the balance of the time the investment is held.

ANALYZING RENTAL PROPERTY

Income property buyers must select investments based on estimates of future vacancies. This is not an exact science, because supply and demand factors can change over time, and development trends may make today's high demand tomorrow's market glut.

The vacancy factor is unavoidably tied to cash flow, since rental income is the essential element for the real estate investor. It is needed to cover operating expenses and debt service, and to build value over time. Income property is most often appraised on the basis of the annual income it produces; thus, a high vacancy rate will directly affect the property's market value.

Keeping in mind the need for positive cash flow, an income property investor can calculate the rental breakeven point. This is a comparison between the required monthly mortgage payment and the rent that will be earned if all units are occupied. The formula is shown in Figure 12.9.

In this example, the monthly payment is $35,207, and the rent for all units equals $45,000. Thus, if 78 percent of all units are rented, that will yield enough cash to make the mortgage payment. If the vacancy rate exceeds 22 percent, then the investor will experience negative cash flow.

In evaluating the income potential and future value of income property, the historical occupancy rate (the opposite of the vacancy rate) is one important test. The formula involves dividing the number of occupied units, by the total units, as demonstrated in Figure 12.10.

The occupancy rate should be reviewed as part of a trend. For example, you are considering investing in a 40-unit apartment complex. Today's

$$\frac{M}{R} = B \qquad\qquad \frac{O}{T} = R$$

M = mortgage payments
R = maximum rent
B = breakeven occupancy

O = occupied units
T = total units
R = occupancy rate

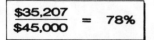

$$\frac{\$35,207}{\$45,000} = 78\%$$

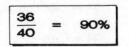

$$\frac{36}{40} = 90\%$$

FIGURE 12.9 Breakeven occupancy.

FIGURE 12.10 Occupancy rate.

occupancy rate is 90 percent. What was it at the end of each quarter, for the last five years? Does today's rate seem high or low in comparison?

A variation of the occupancy rate is the collected rent test. Just because income property is occupied does not necessarily mean that *all* rents are collected each month. Thus, rather than testing for occupancy, it could prove more valuable to test rental payments (dollar amount as a percentage of maximum rent collectible on all units) for the last six months.

Vacancy rate can be expressed in one of three ways: by the number of units, by dollars of rental income, or by the time vacant. Each of these tests reveals information concerning a property's real value to a potential investor, as well as indicating the relative supply and demand conditions in the area.

Figure 12.11 summarizes these three vacancy calculations.

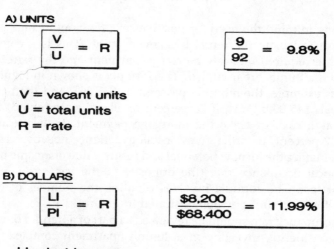

A) UNITS

$$\frac{V}{U} = R \qquad\qquad \frac{9}{92} = 9.8\%$$

V = vacant units
U = total units
R = rate

B) DOLLARS

$$\frac{LI}{PI} = R \qquad\qquad \frac{\$8,200}{\$68,400} = 11.99\%$$

LI = lost income
PI = total potential income
R = rate

C) TIME

$$\frac{M}{Y} = R \qquad\qquad \frac{2}{12} = 16.7\%$$

M = months vacant
Y = full year
R = rate

FIGURE 12.11 Vacancy rate.

APPRAISAL CALCULATIONS

The best-known method for appraising real estate is by market comparison. Most homeowners know how this works. Your home is valued on the basis of the sales prices of similar homes in the same area that were sold during the last year. The range of sales prices limits the potential market value of every property. For example, if you improve your home to add features not found in the typical home in your area, it's unlikely that you will recapture the full cost of those improvements when you sell. The market comparison appraisal sets a natural limit on potential market value.

Two other appraisal methods are used, especially for income properties. First is the *cost approach*. An appraiser bases the estimate on what it would cost today to reproduce a property. This may be based on actual building costs of properties nearby, or on a detailed breakdown of material and labor costs. The estimate is reduced by a depreciation factor, based on the age and condition of the property.

The second income property appraisal method is called the *income approach*. The estimated value of property is based on the income it generates each year, multiplied by a factor based on values of similar income properties.

Example: In one area, the average income property sold during the last year brought a price of $105,000, and the average monthly rental income was $725. The gross rent multiplier in this example was 144.8 (average sales price, divided by average rental income). The formula for this is shown in Figure 12.12.

$$\frac{S}{R} = M$$

S = sales price
R = rent per month
M = multiplier

$$\frac{\$105{,}000}{\$725} = 144.8$$

FIGURE 12.12 Gross rent multiplier.

This multiplier can be applied to appraise similar properties. For example, you own a rental home on which you collect $675 per month in rent. Using the income approach and the multiplier explained above, your home would be valued at $97,740:

$$144.8 \times \$675 = \$97{,}740.$$

While the gross rent multiplier is a device for estimating comparable value, the capitalization rate is a means for calculating growth of an income property's value in the future. The cap rate is a percentage developed from comparison of annual net income to the purchase price.

Example: An income property originally cost $485,000, and generates gross rents of $100,000 per year. However, the recent vacancy factor was 20 percent, so the effective gross income must be reduced to $80,000. Operating expenses were $38,000, and annual net income is $42,000. To summarize the calculation of the annual net:

Gross income	$100,000
Less: Vacancies, 20%	− 20,000
Effective gross income	$ 80,000
Less: Operating expenses	38,000
Annual Net Income	$ 42,000

The cap rate is computed when the annual net income is divided by the original purchase price of $485,000, as shown in Figure 12.13.

Each appraisal method is flawed to a degree, since it concentrates only on certain aspects of a property's value. The market comparison approach may ignore variations in income; and the income approach does not always fairly reflect trends in recent sales.

For this reason, a thorough appraisal often involves calculating estimates of value by all three methods, and then arriving at a weighted appraisal. The weighting of each method allows an appraiser to give more

$$\boxed{\dfrac{I}{P} = R}$$

I = annual net income
P = purchase price
R = cap rate

$$\dfrac{\$42{,}000}{\$485{,}000} = 8.66\%$$

FIGURE 12.13 Capitalization rate.

importance to the method believed to most fairly represent true value. For example, one property is appraised as follows:

METHOD	ESTIMATE
Cost approach	$123,400
Income approach	$128,000
Market approach	$119,000

The appraiser applied the following weight to each of the appraisal methods:

METHOD	WEIGHT
Cost approach	65%
Income approach	15%
Market approach	20%
Total	100%

The weighted appraisal arrives at 100 percent of the estimated value by weighting each of the three methods. The formula for this is illustrated in Figure 12.14.

$$(CP \times C) + (IP \times I) + (MP \times M) = WA$$

CP = cost weight percentage
C = cost basis appraisal
IP = income weight percentage
I = income basis appraisal
MP = market weight percentage
M = market basis appraisal
WA = weighted average

$$(.65 \times \$123,400) + (.15 \times \$128,000) + (.20 \times \$119,000) = \$123,210$$

FIGURE 12.14 Weighted appraisal.

MEASUREMENT OF AREA

Real estate investors must be able to calculate the area of land and, in some instances, the volume of a building, as methods for developing comparative value.

Example: A certain tract of land is advertised as being available for a dollar amount per acre. You have one lot in mind, and you measure the square feet. You must next be able to convert that value to acreage to estimate the price.

Example: You have the legal description of a vacant lot that is triangular. You need to compute the total square feet in order to determine the size home you will be allowed to construct under local building-code rules.

Example: You question the estimates reported in a program's prospectus. The cost of heating and cooling a factory are reported; however, you investigate on your own, and find the cost per cubic yard. Now you must be able to calculate the volume within the building.

Example: You are considering purchasing a small farm. The dimensions of a silo are reported, and you need to determine the capacity, which involves calculating the volume of a cylinder.

In all of these cases, and in numerous other applications, investors must be able to perform two- and three-dimensional measurement calculations. The basic rules for computing the area or volume (summarized below) can be combined or modified so that any land or structural calculation can be performed.

To begin, below is a brief review of conversion values and methods for inches, feet, and yards, as well as for square values:

Conversions	
Feet × 12 = inches	Sq. feet × 144 = sq. inches
$\dfrac{\text{Inches}}{12}$ = feet	$\dfrac{\text{Sq. inches}}{144}$ = sq. feet
Yards × 3 = feet	Sq. yards × 9 = sq. feet
$\dfrac{\text{Feet}}{3}$ = yards	$\dfrac{\text{Sq. feet}}{9}$ = sq. yards
Yards × 36 = inches	Sq. yards × 1296 = sq. inches
$\dfrac{\text{Inches}}{36}$ = yards	$\dfrac{\text{Sq. inches}}{1296}$ = sq. yards

The most often used linear measurement is for the area of a square or rectangle. The length of a lot is multiplied by its width to determine area, as summarized in Figure 12.15.

In the example, the length and width are both expressed in round feet.

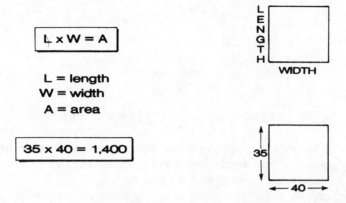

FIGURE 12.15 Area of a rectangle (or square).

However, in actual applications, the size of a lot may be expressed in yards, or in fractional feet or yards. In this case, the square footage must be calculated with converted values.

Converting fractional measurements to decimal value involves finding the common factor. Thus, to compute square feet, it is necessary to convert yards (multiply the number of yards by 3), as well as inches (divide the number of inches by 12).

For example, you want to compute the area in square feet, of a lot with the following measurements:

| Length | 14 yards, 17 inches |
| Width | 9 yards, 2 inches |

To convert to square footage, the yard and inch values must be expressed in full and fractional feet value. In order to multiply, this must be reduced to a decimal equivalent:

Length:

$$14 \text{ yards} \times 3 = 42.00 \text{ feet}$$

$$\frac{17 \text{ inches}}{12} = 1.42 \text{ feet}$$

$$42.00 + 1.42 = 43.42 \text{ feet}$$

Width:

$$9 \text{ yards} \times 3 = 27.00 \text{ feet}$$

$$\frac{2 \text{ inches}}{12} = 0.17 \text{ feet}$$

$$27.00 + 0.17 = 27.17 \text{ feet}$$

Area:

$$43.42 \times 27.17 = 1179.72 \text{ square feet}$$

Equivalent values of squared lots may require conversion from one form to another. That could mean having to convert feet to miles, yards to feet, or square miles to acres, for example.

The squared linear equivalent values of these measurements are:

Equivalent Values		
1 square foot	=	144 square inches
1 square yard	=	9 square feet
1 square mile	=	640 acres
1 acre	=	43,560 square feet

Example: You know the number of square feet in a lot, and must next determine the number of acres this represents. Divide the number of square feet by 43,560, the number of square feet in one acre:

$$\frac{\text{Square feet}}{43,560} = \text{acres.}$$

Example: A lot measures 385 feet by 930 feet. The first step in calculating the number of acres in this lot is to compute the area. Multiply the length by the width:

$$385 \times 930 = 358,050.$$

Divide the square feet by 43,560:

$$\frac{358,050}{43,560} = 8.22 \text{ acres.}$$

The area of a triangle is computed by multiplying two lengths: the base and the height; and then dividing the answer by 2. This calculation is shown in Figure 12.16.

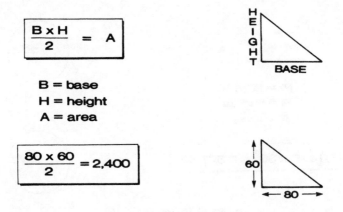

B = base
H = height
A = area

FIGURE 12.16 Area of a triangle.

A trapezoid is a four-sided shape, each side of dissimilar length. The area is computed by adding the top and bottom parallel base lines, dividing by 2, and then multiplying by the height. This is illustrated in Figure 12.17.

To find the area of a circle, it is necessary to use the mathematical value pi, which is approximated as 3.1416. Pi is multiplied by the square of the radius value, which is the distance from the exact center of the circle to the rim. The calculation is shown in Figure 12.18.

In some applications, it will also be necessary to compute the circumference of a circle, or the distance around the outside. To achieve this value, multiply pi by the diameter (the distance from one side of the circle, through the middle to the other side; or twice the value of the radius). The formula for circumference is illustrated in Figure 12.19.

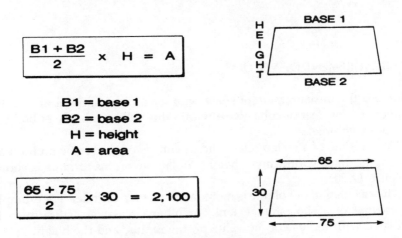

B1 = base 1
B2 = base 2
H = height
A = area

FIGURE 12.17 Area of a trapezoid.

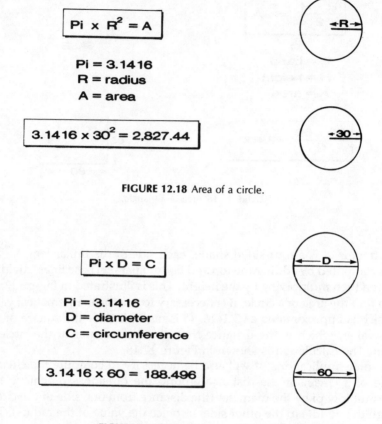

$$Pi \times R^2 = A$$

Pi = 3.1416
R = radius
A = area

$$3.1416 \times 30^2 = 2,827.44$$

FIGURE 12.18 Area of a circle.

$$Pi \times D = C$$

Pi = 3.1416
D = diameter
C = circumference

$$3.1416 \times 60 = 188.496$$

FIGURE 12.19 Circumference of a circle.

MEASUREMENT OF VOLUME

Volume is the measurement of space within a structure. For example, the number of cubic feet or cubic yards within the walls of a home or building represents volume.

The volume of a rectangular solid or cube is calculated by multiplying the length, times width, times height. A sample of this formula is shown in Figure 12.20.

The calculation of volume is more involved for a cylinder. For example, the volume of a silo, storage tank, or other circular structure must be calculated with the use of the value pi, the radius, and the height.

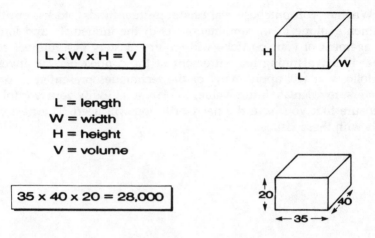

$$L \times W \times H = V$$

L = length
W = width
H = height
V = volume

$$35 \times 40 \times 20 = 28,000$$

FIGURE 12.20 Volume of a rectangular solid.

Example: A storage tank is 35 feet high, and its radius is 30 feet. To estimate its capacity, multiply pi by the radius, squared; and then multiply by the height. The formula is shown in Figure 12.21.

Investing in real estate takes many forms, from direct ownership of a residence or rental property, to participation in a multi-million dollar pool. Investors may purchase raw land, homes, rental, or commercial space. And the calculations required to compare, monitor, and judge investments will demand a wide variety of analyses.

$$Pi \times R^2 \times H = V$$

Pi = 3.1416
R = radius
H = height
V = volume

$$3.1416 \times 30^2 \times 35 = 98,960.4$$

FIGURE 12.21 Volume of a cylinder.

Whether you purchase real estate, mutual funds, stocks, or other investments, alone or in combination, both the immediate and long-term management of your portfolio will require mastery of a number of math skills. When planning for retirement in the context of your investment portfolio, you will apply many of the techniques presented in previous chapters, to calculate future value, to plan and modify your portfolio, and to ensure that you have the net worth you will need. The next chapter deals with these issues.

13

Retirement Math

Figuring out what you will need during your retirement years requires a great deal of assumption. Many of the popular methods for establishing minimum needs in a post-career period may be flawed, unless you calculate actual needs on a realistic basis.

FLAWS IN RETIREMENT ESTIMATES

The flaws in calculation methods arise because future inflation, tax, and income requirement factors are not properly calculated. Keep these points in mind about all retirement estimates:

1. Income might not cease: One popular assumption is that, upon retirement, everyone will desire a life of complete idleness. In reality, few people desire that situation. You might want to continue working and earning a living, perhaps on a part time basis or by starting your own small business.

The popular approach is to assume all income will be derived from investments—interest, dividends, and capital gains. Thus, the assumption is made that every retiree will need to build a relatively large deposit of money, from which earnings can be drawn each month. That assumption will not apply to everyone.

Rather than setting a standard that assumes you will have no earned income, a more realistic approach is to calculate retirement needs with the goal of establishing a desirable degree of financial security and freedom; however, you must also include the possibility that you will continue to work, even if only part-time.

2. Living expenses might not be high: If your financial plan includes the full repayment of a home mortgage, living expenses will be drastically reduced; this factor is often overlooked, notably when retirement needs are based on today's requirements.

One common method for calculating a retirement living expense is to begin with today's income, and multiply that by an assumed inflation factor. This is inaccurate based on the assumption that a mortgage debt, current savings and retirement contributions, the cost of commuting to work, expenses related to raising children, and other currently recurring expenses, will cease in the retirement years.

3. Inflation estimates may be exaggerated: An assumption concerning retirement needs must be adjusted for an inflation allowance. While it's true that the costs of many expenses may be greater in the future, it's inaccurate to base a retirement-needs estimate on the Consumer Price Index. That index is significantly affected by housing and transportation costs; so unless you purchase a new home and a new car every year, your net worth and purchasing power will not be changed by the full CPI rate.

4. Investment value may not be affected by taxes: Taxable investments are usually reduced by your effective tax rate in retirement calculations. For example, you earn 10 percent per year from a mutual fund investment; but your effective tax rate (federal and state) is 30 percent. So the mutual fund is assumed to grow at only 7 percent per year.

Even though taxable income from investments does increase your tax liability, you will not usually sell off part of your account to pay the difference. If that money is set aside for retirement, it's more likely that the full 10 percent will stay on deposit, and the tax burden will be paid from current earnings.

If you absorb an increased tax burden from current income, it is inaccurate to reduce a savings account's future value by the same amount. In this instance, a distinction must be made between growing invested equity, and current income and expenses—a point often overlooked in tax and retirement calculations.

CALCULATING YOUR TAX-DEFERRED EARNINGS

Keeping in mind that many popular retirement assumptions are flawed, any mathematical estimate of your future income and savings requirements must be made with full realization of the income, savings, tax and inflation factors, as they will apply to you.

Tax-deferred earnings are preferable to taxable earnings, as everyone will agree. If you do not participate in a qualified plan, you are eligible for favorable treatment of investments in an Individual Retirement Account (IRA) or, in some instances, in various forms of tax-deferred annuities. You might be able to reduce your taxable income by as much as $2,000 per year deposited in an IRA account.

Even if you do not qualify for deductions of the contributions you make to an IRA, you are still allowed to contribute up to $2,000 and defer taxes on all *earnings* within the account.

Self-employed individuals are allowed to deposit up to 20 percent of their net earnings from business activity, and to deduct contributions from gross income each year. In addition, all Keogh account earnings are tax-deferred.

The maximum contribution is often described as 25 percent of net earnings or $30,000, whichever is less, after contributions have been deducted from net income. This is the same as 20 percent of net.

For example, a self-employed individual reports a net income (revenue less costs and expenses) of $100,000. The maximum Keogh contribution for that year is $20,000. This may be described simply as 20 percent of income, or as 25 percent after allowing for the contribution:

Net income	$100,000
Less: Keogh contribution	− 20,000
Adjusted net income	$ 80,000

Percent contributed:

$$\frac{20,000}{80,000} = 25\%$$

If you qualify for any form of tax-deferred retirement savings, the first assumption you must make is the average annual rate of interest you will earn. While your true rate may vary from one year to the next, a straight estimate is the best you can use today. There is no way to accurately estimate future earnings on investments, since market rates and performance cannot be predicted in the distant future. Using a flat annual rate is an acceptable basis for comparisons and estimates of future net worth.

Even if you estimate high current earnings from investment activity, it will not be accurate to assume that you will be able to earn that rate every year. You cannot lock in a high current rate indefinitely. Thus, in the interest of accuracy, it may be wise to calculate future earnings conservatively.

The first step in calculating future value is to make an assumption concerning the average yearly rate your account will earn. This can be achieved by using the compound interest table for the accumulated value of 1 per period. We recommend basing all assumptions on an annual rate of return, since the compound interest tables assume one deposit per period. Thus, a quarterly interest table is based on four deposits per year; and a monthly table assumes 12 deposits. In most instances, you will base your estimates on contributions of a flat annual amount.

Example: In an IRA account, you deposit $2,000 at the beginning of each year. In order to calculate an assumed annual rate of in-

terest, the annual compounding table will be based on one deposit
per year.

Figure 13.1 shows how one dollar deposited at the beginning
of each year will increase in value in the future. These results are
rounded-out factors from the annual tables for the accumulated
value of 1 per period.

value per $1 saved each year	EARNINGS RATE*		
YEAR	6%	8%	10%
5	5.64	5.87	6.11
10	13.18	14.49	15.94
15	23.28	27.15	31.77
20	36.79	45.76	57.27
25	54.86	73.11	98.35
30	79.06	113.28	164.49
35	111.43	172.32	271.02
40	154.76	259.06	442.59

* assuming annual compounding with interest
payable at the end of each year

FIGURE 13.1   Tax-deferred earnings rate.

To apply these factors per one dollar to the amount you plan to
deposit each year, multiply the amount shown by the amount of
annual deposit. Thus, if you plan to contribute $2,000 per year,
and you plan to begin withdrawals in 30 years, the calculation is:

	Value, 30 Years:		
INTEREST RATE	VALUE PER $1	ANNUAL CONTRIBUTION	TOTAL VALUE
6%	79.06	$2,000	$158,120
7%	113.28	$2,000	$226,560
8%	164.49	$2,000	$328,980

This is as far as most retirement account calculations go. However,
two additional considerations must be met. First is the comparison
between taxable and tax-deferred earnings; and second is the significant value of annual tax liability reduction that results from
making deductible account payments.

AFTER-TAX EARNINGS

It is not accurate to estimate the future value of a taxable investment by deducting the annual tax liability, if that liability will be paid from current income. In reality, the account will be left intact in most instances.

However, it is accurate to estimate the net value of an investment on an after-tax basis, when the investment value will be reduced for annual taxes on that account. And for the purpose of comparison, the tax calculation is worth making.

The formula for computing your after-tax earnings rate involves multiplying the assumed gross rate by the inverse of your effective tax bracket. For example, if you expect to pay 28 percent taxes on your taxable income, the after-tax earnings rate is 72 percent. And if you expect to earn an average of 6 percent per year, the after-tax rate is 4.32 percent. This is summarized in Figure 13.2.

In order to accurately estimate the future value of your account, it will be necessary to calculate each year's compound value. And since a fractional rate is probably not available in a book of compound interest tables, this calculation may have to be done by hand (or, if available, with the use of a computer math program). This is one application in which knowing how to calculate the accumulated value of 1 per period is useful. Because you must base calculations of value on estimates, it is acceptable to avoid manual calculations, and simply round the assumed net rate to the closest one-half percent, and then perform calculations from a book of interest tables.

If you want to compute future estimated value with complete accuracy, it will be necessary to calculate each year's compound value. Recalling the formula for the accumulated value of 1 per period, you must first calculate interest based on the previous year's ending balance; and then to add "1" to the interest earned.

Based on the after-tax earnings rate of 4.32 percent, based on 6 percent and a tax rate of 28 percent, the calculation for 40 years involves 40 steps, as in Table 13.1.

$$R (100 - T) = E$$

R = gross earnings rate
T = tax rate
E = after-tax earnings

$$6\% (100 - 28) = 4.32\%$$

FIGURE 13.2　After-tax earnings rate.

TABLE 13.1   Accumulated Value of 1 per Period

YEAR	DEPOSIT	4.32%	TOTAL	YEAR	DEPOSIT	4.32%	TOTAL
1	1.00	0	1.00	21	1.00	1.33	33.11
2	1.00	.04	2.04	22	1.00	1.43	35.54
3	1.00	.09	3.13	23	1.00	1.54	38.08
4	1.00	.14	4.27	24	1.00	1.65	40.73
5	1.00	.18	5.45	25	1.00	1.76	43.49
6	1.00	.24	6.69	26	1.00	1.88	46.37
7	1.00	.29	7.98	27	1.00	2.00	49.37
8	1.00	.34	9.32	28	1.00	2.13	52.50
9	1.00	.40	10.72	29	1.00	2.27	55.77
10	1.00	.46	12.18	30	1.00	2.41	59.18
11	1.00	.53	13.71	31	1.00	2.56	62.74
12	1.00	.59	15.30	32	1.00	2.71	66.45
13	1.00	.66	16.96	33	1.00	2.87	70.32
14	1.00	.73	18.69	34	1.00	3.04	74.36
15	1.00	.81	20.50	35	1.00	3.21	78.57
16	1.00	.89	22.39	36	1.00	3.39	82.96
17	1.00	.97	24.36	37	1.00	3.58	87.54
18	1.00	1.05	26.41	38	1.00	3.78	92.32
19	1.00	1.14	28.55	39	1.00	3.99	97.31
20	1.00	1.23	30.78	40	1.00	4.20	102.51

This calculation often is performed on the basis of compound gross earnings over a period of years, with the final total then reduced by the average annual tax liability. However, that is inaccurate because the comparison is then not a true taxable and tax-deferred earnings analysis. For example, you calculate that in 30 years, a 6-percent account will earn 79.06 per dollar invested per year. So a $2,000 per year deposit will be worth $158,120. This is reduced by an assumed tax rate of 28 percent:

Gross earnings	$158,120
Less: income tax	− 44,274
After-tax Earnings	$113,846

This is inaccurate because the tax must be paid each and every year. Thus, each year's earnings must be reduced by the effective tax rate; there will be less available to compound during the subsequent year.

The true 30-year net will be $59.18 per dollar invested per year, based on the hand-calculated yearly compound interest at 4.32 percent. So if $2,000 per year is saved, the account will be worth $118,360 on an after-tax basis:

$$\$2,000 \times \$59.18 = \$118,360.$$

value per $1 saved each year *

	6% EARNINGS RATE**		
YEAR	TAX-DEFERRED	TAXABLE	TAX BENEFIT
5	5.64	5.45	.19
10	13.18	12.18	1.00
15	23.28	20.50	2.78
20	36.79	30.78	6.01
25	54.86	43.49	11.37
30	79.06	59.18	19.88
35	111.43	78.57	32.86
40	154.76	102.51	52.25

* assuming annual compounding with interest payable at the end of each year

** reduced 28% to reflect the after-tax rate

FIGURE 13.3   Taxable earnings.

The tax-deferred and taxable compound values of an account at 6 percent per year are shown in Figure 13.3.

ANNUAL TAX REDUCTIONS

In computing the real annual earnings from a tax-deferred contribution, it is necessary to take into account the tax benefits achieved. When you qualify for reduction of gross income, the return you earn in your retirement account comes from two sources:

1. Earnings from interest, dividends, and capital gains;
2. Savings from reduced tax liabilities.

Example: You deposit $2,000 in an IRA account, and do not participate in any other retirement fund. You are allowed to deduct the entire contribution of your federal income tax return, and you pay taxes at the rate of 28 percent of taxable income. The savings in taxes this year equal $560:

$$\$2,000 \times 28\% = \$560.$$

The savings may vary based on marginal rates and the level of deductions you claim. Savings in state income taxes, if applicable, must be computed as well as federal. In some states, the entire amount contributed may not be deductible for the purposes of state income tax. Thus, a separate calculation is required.

To calculate each year's reduction of tax liability, add the amount contributed in your retirement fund, to the reported taxable income on your most recent tax return. Then compute the tax that would have been assessed on that total. Next, deduct the amount of total tax liability you reported. The result is the amount of tax savings for the year. A worksheet for this calculation is shown in Figure 13.4.

To compute the effective annual return earned by making tax-deductible contributions to a retirement account, it is necessary to allow for earnings from interest, dividends, and capital gains, as well as for the yearly tax benefits. In addition, the amount earned should be reduced by a realistic factor for inflation.

This calculation should be performed each year, and the overall results carried forward (or estimated) for each subsequent year between now and retirement. Even though the tax reduction enhances after-tax income, and not the value of your retirement account, the annual savings are a tangible factor. A reduced tax liability increases your spendable income. Thus, you have more available for investment; to reduce debts; and to increase your net worth. Even though the actual cash value of your retirement account will not grow in value due to tax savings, the available cash for other equity-building steps is directly increased.

To compute the annual and to-date net tax-deferred earnings, first write down the amount earned in the account (interest, dividends, and capital gains). Add to that the federal and state tax reductions resulting from deducting annual contributions. Finally, deduct the factor you estimate for

		FEDERAL	STATE
STEP 1	taxable income as reported	$ _____	$ _____
STEP 2	retirement contribution deducted	_____	_____
STEP 3	total (step 1 + step 2)	$ _____	$ _____
STEP 4	tax on step 3	$ _____	$ _____
STEP 5	taxes paid	_____	_____
STEP 6	tax reduction (step 4 − step 5)	$ _____	$ _____

FIGURE 13.4   Retirement plan tax reduction.

	THIS YEAR	TO DATE
STEP 1 net retirement earnings	$_____	$_____
STEP 2 tax reductions: federal state	_____	_____
STEP 3 total earnings (step 1 plus step 2)	$_____	$_____
STEP 4 inflation factor	_____ %	_____ %
STEP 5 net earnings (step 3 x step 4)	$_____	$_____

FIGURE 13.5   Net tax-deferred earnings.

inflation, which reflects the effect of increased prices on future buying power. A worksheet for this computation is shown in Figure 13.5.

A straight calculation of tax-deferred income, at an assumed rate of interest, is not adequate to estimate what will truly be available during retirement. And basing an assumed retirement need on popular assumptions may be flawed as well.

To accurately predict (a) what you will need and (b) what you will have, both the assumption and the calculation must take into account:

1. The question of whether or not you will continue to work after retirement.
2. The reduced monthly requirements you will face after your children have grown, your mortgage is paid off, and other expenses disappear.
3. The true inflation factor you will experience, which is likely to be lower than the Consumer Price Index.
4. The annual savings you generate by reducing tax liabilities as a direct result of making tax-deductible contributions to a retirement account.

In estimating your requirements for invested assets and income during retirement, don't automatically accept the popular assumptions. Question statements to determine whether they are based on a realistic analysis of your likely retirement situation, and develop estimates that match your reasonable expectations. For example, if you believe you will retire and depend entirely on interest, dividends, and capital gains, you will need to build a substantial investment fund; but if you plan to continue working, the entire calculation must be reevaluated.

The calculations associated with retirement math depend on many of the techniques described in previous chapters, especially use of compound interest calculations over a number of years, and considerations for income taxes and inflation.

The ability to use the techniques described in previous chapters, for a number of functions, is a valuable skill for every investor. Several examples of daily math applications for investors will be given in the next chapter.

14

Daily Applications of Math

Investors depend on indicators, trends, ratios, yields, and indices, for even the most basic decisions. The ability to time transactions and select the best products for your portfolio requires that you be comfortable with the principles supporting the investor's task.

The ability to comprehend and then apply the mathematical principles required for investing must not be thought of as the end result, but as part of the process. It's one of the tools every investor must use. However, with the availability of low-cost home computers and programs supporting portfolio analysis, this important caveat is easily overlooked.

STAYING IN CONTROL

If the principles of investment math are applied without the required risk standards and financial planning goals every investor needs, then they are not being used in an appropriate context. Control is the central idea that must support every strategy you apply in managing your investments. The decision to buy or sell securities, evaluate companies, and determine the significance of a trend are aided by application of math. But even with the most advanced form of analysis, you cannot achieve your planning goals unless you set limits. This applies both to your overall financial position and to the level of risk you accept.

Investors want to be in control. This idea will be elusive for anyone who does not recognize the nature of the market, or accept the limited range of matters over which actions can be controlled. There are three principles that will help you to achieve and maintain control.

The first principle relates to validity. In attempting to control and define, you cannot always depend on information supplied from others. For example, a comparison between two different investments might be made on the assumption that projections are provided on a similar basis. However, the underlying assumptions relating to two investments can be entirely different. The mathematical skill required of every investor is not limited to mastering formulas or compound interest tables; it extends to ensuring that the premise of a comparison is correct.

Every aspect of control requires comparison. You compare one company to another to judge fundamental strength; you watch charting patterns from week to week, to spot buy and sell signals; and you compare yields in two or more fixed-income securities.

In each case, you must ask: How accurate are my comparisons? If you want to control the decision-making process, the first mathematical principle must be:

The comparison must be valid in order for an analysis to hold any significance.

Example: An investor has narrowed his selection to two companies; he will purchase stock in only one. He compares fundamental indicators for each one, studying trends in sales and profits. However, the standards for the two companies are dissimilar, because they operate in extremely different industry environments. The line-by-line comparison of profit yield and sales levels do not grant the investor the desired valid comparison.

Example: A technician tracks price movement for several stocks over a six-month period. However, the price movement trends in certain industries (and at certain times) are separate and distinct. A comparison of price movements within one company might hold significance for the technician. But a comparison between companies in different industries might not be valid.

Example: An investor compares nominal yield on several bonds. The purpose: To select the bond that will yield the highest rate of interest. But this approach does not take into account the different safety levels or ratings of various bonds; guarantees concerning safety; financial strength of the issuer; current discount or premium; time remaining until maturity; or overall market trends for interest rates.

If you want to remain in control, mathematical skill by itself is not enough. That skill must be applied within a proper comparison. The second principle to follow is:

The validity of a comparison must depend on the risk and safety standards you set.

There is no point in using someone else's assumptions, if those assumptions conflict with the risk standards you have established. Control depends on first ensuring the approach you take in evaluating risk. And making the best decision is always a matter of timing.

You can expect only to control the selection standards you use. There is no absolutely sure way to eliminate all of the risks inherent in the investing process. You can apply mathematical processes to manage risk, on the assumption that you begin by defining what is acceptable.

No investment is risk-free; and no investor can expect to gain a profit from every decision made. Successful investors understand that losses will occur, and they are willing to live with those losses. They know that their approach will also produce gains, perhaps more gains than losses. And because they have defined an acceptable level of risk, the losses they experience are not devastating. The third principle is:

Losses are acceptable, as long as the initial risks of the investment were acceptable, too.

Most investors would define their experience as successful as long as their gains were greater than their losses. While the pure profit-and-loss analysis is certainly a valid part of portfolio management, the definition of success must go beyond this. You should ask yourself these questions:

1. Does my current portfolio conform to my financial plan?
2. Am I investing to meet long-term goals?
3. Do I understand all of the risks to which I'm exposed in my portfolio, and am I willing to accept those risks?
4. Have I made a distinction between funds invested for long-term growth, and for short-term speculation or income?
5. In selecting investments today, do I apply my personal risk standards as a basic premise of the selection?

APPLYING YOUR OWN STANDARDS

Defining an acceptable level of risk and developing a farsighted financial plan are only the starting points. Using those standards to invest proves much more difficult. An investor might accept the premise, but can that same investor put it into practice? A large portion of investors tends to act on "opportunity" rather than within the defined limitations of a plan.

Example: An investor puts a lot of effort into developing a personal financial plan. This includes specific short-term and long-term goals; identification of acceptable risk levels; and criteria for buying and selling. His primary interest is the stock market. In spite of the extensive planning and definition, however, he does not apply his standards in actually selecting investments. When his stock broker phones and recommends a "hot" stock, he purchases shares without any form of analysis.

There's no point in putting time and energy into the development of
an intelligent investment standard, unless it's also put into practice. You
can avoid investing in response to so-called opportunities, by demanding
to see research, financial information, and other material you need in order
to apply your decision tests—before you make your decision.

As a second step, before you invest, ask this question: How does this
investment suit my goals, and how does it fit with my personal risk standards? At this point, a rather simple mathematical test can be applied. An
investment falls above or below an imaginary line you create. You will
purchase securities only when the tests you apply place them at or above
your line.

You might find it necessary to alter your standards, change assumptions, or accept new goals. Developing initial risk and planning criteria is
essential, but circumstances can change, or you might find that your plan
is unrealistic. Some examples requiring a change in your initial premise:

1. Your economic status changes: At the time you develop your financial
plan, you operate with a given series of assumptions. These may be correct
at that time, but could change later, as the direct result of a change in your
economic status. When you get married, have children, buy a home, inherit
money, start your own business, or go through any other radical change,
your plan must be altered as well.

A common mistake investors make is failing to reevaluate their financial
priorities when their economic status changes.

2. Your perception of risk changes: Directly related to your economic
status is the perception of risk. You might apply one standard today, only
to apply an entirely different one next year.

As the amount of money you have at work in invested assets grows,
you will also undergo a change in perception of risk. And with actual
experience, your understanding of the risk equation develops into something other than what it was in the past.

All of these possibilities point to the need for continuing evaluation,
questioning of your own assumptions and standards, and application of
updated risk criteria.

3. Your assumptions are flawed: Risk standards are developed on the
basis of assumptions. For example, you believe the stock market acts in
certain ways, that the economy undergoes changes in a specific sequence,
and interest rates rise or fall within a specific range. In addition, you believe
you can tolerate certain risks, while you cannot tolerate others. All of these
assumptions could prove to be wrong in the future.

4. Your standards are unrealistic: Some investors discover that their standards have been set too high. This is easy to spot. If you cannot find any investments that meet your criteria, that means that either you cannot afford the risks that exist in the market, or you have set standards unrealistically high.

For example, one investor determined that his portfolio must be invested in insured accounts; yield 12 percent or more; and be highly liquid. However, finding one investment that met all of these standards was not possible. The investor had to change or give up one or more of the standards; or simply not invest money. No one of the criteria is necessarily wrong; but in combination, they cannot be fulfilled.

5. Your goals are unrealistic: If your risk standards and goals are in conflict, something has to give way. You might not be able to meet an aggressive goal in a short period of time, with a highly conservative approach to risk.

> *Example*: One investor wants to pay off his home mortgage in ten
> years or less, with additional payments to principal derived from
> current investment profits. However, he is a very cautious investor,
> and the required cash from profits doesn't materialize. In this case,
> the investor must either lengthen the deadline for achieving the
> goal, or change risk standards.

MATH IN CONTEXT

A lot of emphasis is placed on immediate profit, on formula selection, and non-criteria investing. For example:

- A particular investment is promoted only on the basis of potential profits; the question of risk is ignored or played down.
- A technician, seeing a pattern in a chart, decides it's time to buy. However, many other signals indicate it might be time to stay out of the market. Right after the purchase, the market falls and the investor's stock loses several points.
- An investor purchases shares in a company because his stockbroker recommends the decision. This is done without reviewing any fundamental or technical information.

In each case, an obvious flaw prevents the investor from making an *informed* decision. Many promoters address the potential of yield without mentioning the risks that are involved. Technicians may pore over charts looking for profit opportunities, but ignore the overall market conditions —and those conditions might have more effect on price movement than the charts show. And when an investor bases decisions on outside advice, there can be no expectation of consistent or profitable results. No criteria are being used at all.

Some investors will argue that a financial planner or stockbroker is best suited to advise them, because they do understand the individual's goals or risk standards. In practice, however, any outside adviser will determine what recommendations to make, using his or her own assumptions, and not anyone else's. No one else can manage a portfolio, or recommend, with the same degree of care and diligence, as you can exercise for yourself.

Mathematical processes are essential in every form of analysis. And the skill to comprehend and apply those processes will help investors achieve the goals they have set. But beyond that, an intelligent program must balance potential profits with risk, all within the limits you set for yourself. Investing success comes not from mastering techniques and then applying them blindly; it comes from being able to use the techniques to evaluate and monitor your portfolio. Success doesn't mean winning all of the time; it means that every decision is made with a complete understanding of the risks involved.

Appendix

Investment Ratios and Formulas

CHAPTER 1: THE TIME VALUE OF MONEY

Rule of 72

$$\frac{72}{r} = Y,$$

where

    r = interest rate,
    Y = years required to double principal.

Interest Calculation

$$P \times R \times T = I,$$

where

    P = principal,
    R = interest rate,
    T = time,
    I = interest.

Daily Compounding

$$\frac{A}{365} = D,$$

where

    A = annual rate,
    D = daily rate.

Monthly Compounding

$$\frac{A}{12} = M,$$

where

    A = annual rate,
    M = monthly rate.

Quarterly Compounding

$$\frac{A}{4} = Q,$$

where

    A = annual rate,
    Q = quarterly rate.

Semiannual Compounding

$$\frac{A}{2} = S,$$

where

    A = annual rate,
    S = semiannual rate.

Accumulated Value of 1 (dollar amount)
$$D(1 + r)^n = AV,$$

where

D = deposit,
r = interest rate,
n = number of periods,
AV = accumulated value of 1.

Accumulated Value of 1 per Period (dollar amount)
$$D\left(\frac{(1 + r)^n - 1}{r}\right) = AV,$$

where

D = deposits,
n = number of periods,
r = interest rate,
AV = accumulated value of 1 per period.

Present Value of 1 (dollar amount)
$$\frac{1}{(1 + r)^n} = PV,$$

where

r = interest rate,
n = number of periods,
PV = present value of 1.

Sinking Fund Payments (dollar amount)
$$A\left[\frac{1}{((1 + r)^n - 1)/r}\right] = D,$$

where

A = target amount,
n = number of periods,
r = interest rate,
D = deposits.

Present Value of 1 per Period (dollar amount)
$$W\left[\left(1 - \frac{1}{(1 + r)^n}\right)\Big/r\right] = PV,$$

where

W = withdrawal amount,
r = interest rate,
n = number of periods,
PV = present value of 1 per period.

Amortization Payments (dollar amount)
$$B\left(\frac{1}{PV^n}\right) = P,$$

where

B = balance,
PV = present value of 1 per period,
n = number of periods,
P = amortization payments.

CHAPTER 2: MASTERING INTEREST TABLES

Accumulated Value of 1 (table factor)
$$(1 + r)^n = AV,$$

where

r = interest rate,
n = number of periods,
AV = factor, accumulated value of 1.

Accumulated Value of 1 per Period (table factor)
$$1 + (PF (1 + r)) = AVP,$$

where

PF = previous factor,
r = interest rate,
AVP = factor, accumulated value of 1 per period.

Present Value of 1 (table factor)
$$\left(\frac{1}{1 + r}\right)^n = PV,$$

where

r = interest rate,
n = number of
 periods,
PV = factor, present
 value of 1.

Sinking Fund Payments (table
 factor)
$$\frac{1}{AVP} = SF,$$

where

AVP = factor,
accumulated
value of 1
per period,

SF = factor,
sinking fund
payments.

Present Value of 1 per Period (table factor)
$$PV^1 + \ldots PV^n = PVP,$$

where

PV = factor, present value of 1,
n = number of periods,
PVP = factor, present value of 1 per period.

Amortization Payments (table factor)
$$\frac{1}{PVP} = AP,$$

where

PVP = factor, present value of 1 per period,
AP = factor, amortization payments.

CHAPTER 3:　RATES OF RETURN

Annualized Return
$$\frac{Y}{M} \times 12 = A,$$

where

Y = yield,
M = months held,
A = annualized
return.

Yield on Common Stock
$$\frac{D}{P} = Y,$$

where

D = annual
dividend,
P = current market
price,
Y = yield on
common stock.

Return on Invested Capital
$$\frac{N + I}{E + B} = R$$

where

N = net income,
I = interest
expense,
E = shareholders'
equity,
B = par value of
long-term
bonds,
R = return on
invested capital.

Discount Yield

$$\frac{D}{F} \times \frac{360}{M} = Y,$$

where

D = discount amount,
F = face amount,
M = days to maturity,
Y = discount yield.

CHAPTER 4:   TAXES AND INFLATION

Breakeven

$$\frac{I}{100 - T} = B,$$

where

I = inflation rate,
T = tax rate,
B = breakeven.

CHAPTER 5:   FUNDAMENTAL ANALYSIS

Price/Earnings Ratio

$$\frac{MP}{EPS} = PE$$

where

MP = market price,
EPS = earnings per share,
PE = price/earnings ratio.

Primary Earnings per Share

$$\frac{NE}{OS} = EPS$$

where

NE = net earnings (net income less preferred dividends),
OS = outstanding shares of common stock,
EPS = primary earnings per share.

Fully Diluted Earnings per Share

$$\frac{NE + CV}{OSC} = FD$$

where

NE = net earnings,
CV = conversion value,
OSC = outstanding shares of common stock,
FD = fully diluted earnings per share.

Payout Ratio

$$\frac{CD}{NI - PD} = PR,$$

where

CD = dividends on common stock,
NI = net income,
PD = dividends on preferred stock,
PR = payout ratio.

Current Ratio

$$\frac{CA}{CL} = CR,$$

where

CA = current assets,
CL = current liabilities,
CR = current ratio.

Quick-assets Ratio

$$\frac{CA - I}{CL} = QA,$$

where

CA = current assets,
I = inventory,
CL = current liabilities,
QA = quick assets ratio.

Working Capital Turnover

$$\frac{GS}{CA - CL} = WC,$$

where

GS = gross sales,
CA = current assets,
CL = current liabilities,
WC = working capital turnover.

Debt/Equity Ratio

$$\frac{L}{TN} = DE,$$

where

L = total liabilities,
DE = debt/equity ratio,
TN = net worth.

Bond Ratio

$$\frac{B}{TC} = R,$$

where

B = bonds,
TC = total capitalization,
R = bond ratio.

Preferred Stock Ratio

$$\frac{P}{TC} = R,$$

where

P = preferred stock,
TC = total capitalization,
R = preferred stock ratio.

Common Stock Ratio

$$\frac{C + S + E}{TC} = R,$$

where

C = common stock,
S = capital surplus,
E = retained earnings,
TC = total capitalization,
R = common stock ratio.

Interest Coverage

$$\frac{E}{I} = IC,$$

where

E = earnings before interest and taxes,
I = bond interest,
IC = interest coverage.

Preferred Dividend Coverage

$$\frac{NI}{PD} = PDC,$$

where

NI = net income,
PD = preferred stock dividends,
PDC = preferred dividend coverage.

Expense Ratio

$$\frac{CG + OE + D}{NS} = ER,$$

where

CG = cost of goods sold,
OE = operating expenses,
D = depreciation,
NS = net sales,
ER = expense ratio.

Margin of Profit

$$\frac{OI}{NS} = MP,$$

where

OI = operating income,
NS = net sales,
MP = margin of profit.

Book Value per Share

$$\frac{C + S + E - I}{OS} = BV,$$

where

C = common stock,
S = capital surplus,
E = retained earnings,
I = intangible assets,
OS = number of outstanding shares,
BV = book value per share.

CHAPTER 6: TECHNICAL ANALYSIS

Breadth-of-the-market Index

$$\frac{A - D}{T} = B,$$

where

A = advancing issues,
D = declining issues,
T = total issues,
B = breadth-of-the-market index.

Absolute Breadth Index

$$A - D = B,$$

where

A = advancing issues,
D = declining issues,
B = absolute breadth index.

Advancing Issues

$$\frac{A}{T} = N,$$

where

A = advancing issues,
T = total issues traded,
N = trend.

Declining Issues

$$\frac{D}{T} = N,$$

where

D = declining issues,
T = total issues traded,
N = trend.

New High/New Low Ratio

$$\frac{NH}{NL} = R,$$

where

NH = number of issues with new high prices,
NL = number of issues with new low prices,
R = new high/new low ratio.

Cash-to-assets Ratio

$$\frac{C}{A} = R,$$

where

C = cash and cash equivalents,
A = total fund assets,
R = cash-to-assets ratio.

Large Block Ratio

$$\frac{B}{V} = R,$$

where

B = volume in block trading,
V = total volume,
R = large block ratio.

Volatility

$$\frac{H - L}{L} = V,$$

where

H = high price,
L = low price,
V = volatility.

CHAPTER 7:   APPLYING TECHNICAL INDICATORS

Moving Average

a) $\dfrac{F}{D} = A,$

b) $\dfrac{F - 1 + (F + 1)}{D} = A,$

where

$$F = \text{field},$$
$$D = \text{number of periods in field},$$
$$F - 1 = \text{oldest day in field},$$
$$F + 1 = \text{replacement day},$$
$$A = \text{moving average}.$$

Exponent

$$\dfrac{2}{F} = E,$$

where

$$F = \text{field},$$
$$E = \text{exponent}.$$

CHAPTER 9:   MATH FOR THE OPTIONS MARKET

Delta

$$\dfrac{O}{S} = D,$$

where

$$O = \text{dollar change in option premium},$$
$$S = \text{dollar change in stock's market price},$$
$$D = \text{delta}.$$

Intrinsic Value (Calls)

$$MV - SP = I,$$

where

$$MV = \text{market value above striking price},$$
$$SP = \text{striking price},$$
$$I = \text{intrinsic value}.$$

CHAPTER 10: MATH FOR THE BOND MARKET

Present Value of a Bond

$$\frac{FV}{(1 + r)^t} = PV,$$

where

FV = face value,
r = interest rate per half-year,
t = number of half-year periods,
PV = present value of a bond.

Current Yield

$$\frac{C}{P} = Y,$$

where

C = coupon amount,
P = today's price,
Y = current yield.

Yield to Maturity

a) $$\frac{FV - DP}{M} = APY,$$

b) $APY + C = ANI,$

c) $$\frac{ANI}{P} = A,$$

d) $$\frac{ANI}{P - APY} = B,$$

e) $$\frac{A + B}{2} = YTM,$$

where

FV = face (par) value,
DP = discount or premium,
M = years to maturity,
APY = average per year,
C = coupon amount,
ANI = annual net income,
P = purchase price,
A = yield A,
B = yield B,
YTM = yield to maturity.

CHAPTER 11: MATH FOR MUTUAL FUNDS

Weighted Return

$$\left(\frac{M1}{T} \times r\right) + \left(\frac{M2}{T} \times r\right) = W,$$

where

$M1$ = months in first period,
$M2$ = months in second period,
T = total holding period,
r = rate of return,
W = weighted return.

Average Basis

a) $$D \times \frac{M}{12} = A,$$

b) $$A + \ldots A = B,$$

where

D = amount deposited,
M = months held,
A = average initial value,
B = average basis.

Net Asset Value

$$\frac{MV + C}{S} = NAV,$$

where

MV = market value of invested assets,
C = cash on hand,
S = number of shares outstanding,
NAV = net asset value.

Expense Ratio

a) $$\frac{A1 + A2}{2} = ANA,$$

b) $$\frac{E}{ANA} = ER,$$

where

$A1$ = assets, beginning of year,
$A2$ = assets, end of year,
ANA = average net assets,
E = expenses,
ER = expense ratio.

Cash-to-assets Ratio

$$\frac{C}{P} = R,$$

where

C = cash on hand,
P = portfolio value,
R = cash/assets ratio.

CHAPTER 12:   MATH FOR REAL ESTATE INVESTMENTS

Cash-on-cash Return
$$\frac{CF}{CI} = CC,$$

where
    CF = cash flow,
    CI = cash invested,
    CC = cash on cash
           return.

Equity Return
$$\frac{C + P}{I} = R,$$

where
    C = cash-basis
        income,
    P = payments to
        principal,
    I = investment,
    R = equity return.

Equity Dividend Rate
$$\frac{CF}{I} = R,$$

where
    CF = cash flow
         before taxes,
    I = investment,
    R = equity
        dividend rate.

Debt Coverage Ratio
$$\frac{I}{P} = R,$$

where
    I = net operating
        income,
    P = annual loan
        payment,
    R = debt coverage
        ratio.

Average Interest Rate

$$\left(\frac{P1}{P1 + P2} \times R1\right) + \left(\frac{P2}{P1 + P2} \times R2\right) = A,$$

where
$P1$ = principal balance, loan 1,
$P2$ = principal balance, loan 2,
$R1$ = interest rate, loan 1,
$R2$ = interest rate, loan 2,
A = average interest rate.

Loan-to-balance Ratio

$$\frac{B}{A} = R,$$

where
B = loan balance,
A = appraised value,
R = loan-to-balance
       ratio.

Mortgage Constant

$$\frac{P}{L} = C,$$

where
P = annual
       payments,
L = original loan
       amount,
C = mortgage
       constant.

Refinancing Absorption

$$\frac{C}{S} = R,$$

where
C = cost of
       refinancing,
S = savings per
       month,
R = refinancing
       absorption.

Breakeven Occupancy
$$\frac{M}{R} = B,$$

where

M = mortgage
     payment,
R = maximum rent,
B = breakeven
     occupancy.

Occupancy Rate
$$\frac{O}{T} = R,$$

where

O = occupied units,
T = total units,
R = occupancy rate.

Vacancy Rate (units)
$$\frac{V}{U} = R,$$

where

V = vacant units,
U = total units,
R = vacancy rate
     (units).

Vacancy Rate (dollars)
$$\frac{LI}{PI} = R,$$

where

LI = lost income,
PI = total potential
     income,
R = vacancy rate
     (dollars).

Vacancy Rate (time)
$$\frac{M}{Y} = R,$$

where

M = months vacant,
Y = full year (or
     other period),
R = vacancy rate
     (time).

Gross Rent Multiplier
$$\frac{S}{R} = M,$$

where

S = sales price,
R = rent per month,
M = gross rent
     multiplier.

Capitalization Rate
$$\frac{I}{P} = R,$$

where

I = annual net
     income,
P = purchase price,
R = capitalization
     rate.

Weighted Appraisal
$$(CP \times C) + (IP \times I) + (MP \times M) = WA,$$

where

CP = cost weight percentage,
C = cost basis appraisal,
IP = income weight percentage,
I = income basis appraisal,
MP = market weight percentage,
M = market basis appraisal,
WA = weighted appraisal.

Area of a Rectangle (or Square)
$$L \times W = A,$$

where

L = length,
W = width,
A = area of a rectangle (or square).

Area of a Triangle
$$\frac{B \times H}{2} = A,$$

where

B = base,
H = height,
A = area of a triangle.

Area of a Trapezoid
$$\frac{B1 + B2}{2} \times H = A,$$

where

$B1$ = base 1,
$B2$ = base 2,
H = height,
A = area of a trapezoid.

Area of a Circle
$$Pi \times R^2 = A,$$

where
    Pi = 3.1416,
    R = radius,
    A = area of a circle.

Circumference of a Circle
    $Pi \times D = C,$

where

    Pi = 3.1416,
    D = diameter,
    C = circumference
        of a circle.

Volume of a Rectangular Solid
    $L \times W \times H = V,$

where

    L = length,
    W = width,
    H = height,
    V = volume of a
        rectangle.

Volume of a Cylinder
    $Pi \times R^2 \times H = V,$

where

    Pi = 3.1416,
    R = radius,
    H = height,
    V = volume of a
        cylinder.

CHAPTER 13:   RETIREMENT MATH

After-tax Earnings Rate
    $R (100 - T) = E,$

where

    R = gross earnings rate,
    T = tax rate,
    E = after-tax earnings rate.

Glossary

absolute breadth index A variation of the breadth-of-the-market test; the number of daily issues reporting a decline in price is deducted from the number of issues advancing; the result is reported as a plus or minus number.

accumulated value of 1 The compounded value of a single deposit, based on a number of periods, a rate of interest, and a compounding method.

accumulated value of 1 per period The compounded value of a series of deposits, based on a number of periods, a rate of interest, and a compounding method.

adjusted basis In real estate, the purchase price plus closing costs and improvements, less depreciation.

adjusted sales price In real estate, the contract sales price plus closing costs and fixing-up expenses.

advance/decline noncumulative trend A technical indicator reporting the daily net change in advancing and declining issues. To calculate, subtract the number of declining issues from the number of advancing issues; and divide the net difference by the total number of issues traded.

advancing issues A trend percentage, computed by dividing the number of advancing issues by total issues traded.

after-tax cash flow In real estate, rent income less operating expenses, mortgage payments, and income taxes, plus depreciation.

after-tax earnings rate The net percentage earned after deducting the tax rate from 100 percent. To calculate, divide after-tax earnings by gross earnings.

after-tax profits The amount of profit, after deducting all costs, expenses, and taxes.

amortization payments An amount of equal periodic payments required to retire a debt over an assumed number of periods, based on an assumed rate of interest and compounding method.

annual compounding A method of paying interest at the stated annual rate, but with subsequent years' interest based on principal plus accumulated interest. (Contrast to *simple interest*.)

annual factor A factor developed to compute an abbreviated form of annualization. To calculate, divide 12 by the number of months in the holding period.

annualized return The percentage earned, modified to reflect a full year's rate or the rate earned during the average year. The yield is divided by the number of months held, and the result is multiplied by 12.

area In real estate, the size of land in terms of square feet, used to estimate income per foot as a means for comparison between properties:
a) Rectangle or square: Multiply length by width.
b) Triangle: Multiply base by height; divide the result by 2.
c) Trapezoid: Add top and bottom parallel base and divide the total by 2; multiply the result by the height.
d) Circle: Multiply Pi (3.1416) by the square of the radius.

at the money In options trading, descriptive of the condition in which current market value of stock is equal to the striking price of an option.

average basis The basis in an investment, computed when amounts and timing of deposits are dissimilar. To calculate, each deposit amount is multiplied by the number of months held, and the total is divided by 12 (annualized basis). The results of these calculations are summed to arrive at the average rate.

average interest rate In real estate, the calculation of interest rate when two mortgages are outstanding on a single property. The principal of each loan is divided by the total debt, and the result is multiplied by the rate. The results of these calculations are summed to arrive at the average rate.

beta A test of volatility, comparing a single stock's price trend, in relation to the overall market. Beta can be calculated only when a stock's price moves in the same general direction as the market.

block trade An institutional trade, consisting of 10,000 shares or a number of shares divisible by 10,000.

bond ratio A test to determine the portion of total capital represented by long-term debt capitalization. To calculate, divide the current liability for bonds, by total capital.

book value per share The liquidation value of a company, reflecting the dollar value per share of common stock. To calculate, add common stock, capital surplus, and retained earnings; subtract the value of any intangible assets; and divide the net by the number of outstanding shares of common stock.

breadth-of-the-market A technical trend reflecting the daily trend in advancing and declining issues. To calculate, subtract the number of declining issues from the number of advancing issues; divide the net by the total number of issues traded. *See also* **Advance/decline noncumulative trend.**

breakaway gap In charting, a gap between the trading range from one day to the next, and establishing a price movement away from a previous trading range.

breakeven occupancy In real estate, the percentage of units that must be occupied to cover debt service. To calculate, divide the mortgage payment by the maximum rental income, assuming full occupancy.

breakeven The amount of return that must be earned to retain principal value, after allowing for the effects of income tax and inflation. To calculate, divide an assumed rate of inflation by after-tax yield (100 less effective tax rate).

breakout pattern In charting, a price trend moving above or below a previously established trading range.

capitalization The sum of all debt and equity capital available to a company. Equity capitalization consists of common and preferred stock.

capitalization rate In real estate, a method for estimating growth in the value of an income property. To calculate, divide annual net income (after deducting a vacancy factor), by the purchase price.

cash-on-cash return In real estate, an assumed yield based strictly on cash. To calculate, divide annual cash payments by the amount of cash invested.

cash-to-assets ratio A mutual fund test comparing relative liquidity, used to judge sentiment among mutual fund managers. To calculate, add cash and cash equivalents; and divide by total fund assets.

circumference of a circle The distance around the edge of a circular property. To calculate, multiply Pi (3.1416) by the diameter.

common stock ratio A capitalization test, in which the value of common stockholders' equity is expressed as a percentage of the total capital. To calculate, add the value of common stock, capital surplus, and retained earnings; and divide the sum by total capital.

compound interest Interest on principal and interest; the periodic payment of interest on a previous balance, creating an accelerated rate of growth over time.

confidence theory The belief that overall investor confidence dictates immediate and future price trends.

constant-dollar plan A formula technique, involving investment of the same amount at periodic intervals.

constant ratio plan A formula technique, involving maintenance of an identical percentage in two or more choices of investments.

constant share plan A formula technique, involving regular periodic purchase of an identical number of shares in stock or mutual funds.

contrarian An investor who watches general market sentiment, believing that the majority is usually wrong, and invests in opposition to that sentiment.

conversion value The parity value of convertible bonds or preferred stock, expressed in terms of shares of the underlying common stock.

cost approach An appraisal method in which a property's replacement or reproduction cost is calculated, and then adjusted for a depreciation factor based on age and condition.

coupon rate The stated interest rate paid to bondholders; the nominal yield.

cumulative volume index A technical trend that tracks a running total of daily volume. To calculate, subtract the day's volume in declining issues from the volume in advancing issues; and add the net difference to the cumulative total.

current assets A company's cash and other assets that are usually converted to cash within 12 months.

current liabilities A company's debts that will become payable within the next 12 months.

current ratio A test of a company's ability to manage its working capital. To calculate, divide current assets by current liabilities.

current yield The rate of return being earned, based on the current value of a bond or stock. It is calculated by dividing the coupon rate on a bond or the annual dividend on a stock, by the current value.

cushion theory *See* **Short-interest theory.**

daily compounding A method of compounding interest, in which the annual rate is divided by 365 (or by 360), to arrive at a daily rate.

debt capitalization Capitalization obtained through the issuance of bonds and other debt instruments.

debt coverage ratio A factor showing the adequacy of income to cover debt service. To calculate, divide net operating income by the amount of annual loan payments.

debt/equity ratio A capitalization test, comparing debt to net worth. To compute, divide total liabilities by net worth.

declining issues A trend percentage, computed by dividing the number of declining issues by total issues traded.

Delta A comparison between price movements in a stock and in related options, used to identify buy and sell opportunities in the options market. To calculate, divide the unit change in option premium value, by the unit change in value of the underlying stock.

diagonal spread The simultaneous purchase and sale of an equal number of options of the same class, when the striking price and expiration dates are different on each side.

diameter Any straight line drawn through the center from one edge of a circle to the other.

discount bond A bond purchased below, or currently valued below its face value.

discount yield The calculation of yield on short-term debt securities purchased at discount. To calculate as a percent, divide the amount of the discount by face value; multiply the result by the portion of year remaining until maturity (360 divided by the number of days to maturity date).

dividend yield *See* **Yield on common stock**.

dollar-cost averaging A formula technique, involving a regular periodic investment of a set amount of money, that results in the average cost per unit being lower than the average of the prices paid.

double bottom In charting, a double test of a stock's support level.

double top In charting, a double test of a stock's resistance level.

Dow Theory A belief that future primary price movements of the industrial averages can be predicted, based on trends corroborated by primary price movements in the utility and transportation averages.

earnings per share *See* **Primary earnings per share**.

earnings-per-share ranking A trend reported by *Investor's Daily* that ranks each stock from 0 to 99, based on earnings growth over the past five years.

efficient market theory A theory stating that the current market value of stocks reflects investor reaction to all generally known fundamental and technical information.

Elliott Wave Principle A theory stating that specific mathematical relationships can be used to predict price trends in the market. The Principle is based on studies of the Fibonacci Sequence in relation to long-term price movements.

equity capitalization Capitalization obtained through the sale of shares of stock.

equity dividend rate In real estate, a comparison of pre-tax cash earned, to cash basis. To calculate, divide cash flow before income taxes, by the amount invested.

equity return In real estate, a comparison between equity and the original investment. To calculate, add cash-basis income to payments assigned to principal; and divide the total by the original investment.

exercise In options trading, the act of purchasing 100 shares per call contract held; or of selling 100 shares per put contract held.

exhaustion gap In charting, the last phase of a price trend, followed by an island (a period of relatively stable price range), and likely to end with a price movement in the opposite direction.

expense (*also* operating) ratio (1) In fundamental analysis, the reported relationship between the cost and expense of conducting business, and gross income generated. To calculate, add cost of goods sold, operating expenses, and depreciation; and divide the total by net sales. (2) In mutual fund reporting, a reported level of expenses assessed. To calculate, divide expenses by average fund assets.

expiration In options trading, the end of a contract's life; the date on which the option becomes worthless.

exponent The factor used in exponential moving average. To calculate, divide 2 by the number of fields in the moving average.

exponential moving average A simplified method used to calculate moving average. An exponent is used to calculate the latest addition's effect on the total, adding greater weight to the latest factor.

Fibonacci Sequence An indefinite series of integers, in which each number is equal to the sum of the preceding two numbers. *Example*: $1 + 2 = 3; 2 + 3 = 5; 3 + 5 = 8$. This sequence recurs in nature, and serves as the basis for the Elliott Wave Principle.

fully diluted earnings per share A variation of primary earnings per share expanded to assume net earnings if convertible rights are exercised.

fundamental analysis A method of evaluating companies and their stock, based strictly on financial information and related factual conditions, such as product development, changes in management, and other situations expected to impact future sales and profits.

gap pattern A price movement in which a price gap is created between trading ranges of two subsequent days.

gross profit Profit earned by deducting direct costs from sales, but before deducting operating expenses, interest, or taxes.

gross rent multiplier In real estate, a factor used to establish appraised value of income properties. The multiplier is calculated for similar properties, and applied to a subject property. To calculate, divide other properties' sales price by the rent per month.

head-and-shoulders pattern In charting, a bearish trend characterized by three upward movements, with offsetting downward adjustments. The second of three phases (the head) exceeds the first and third (shoulders). *See also* **Inverted head-and-shoulders pattern**.

hedge A strategy in which one investment position protects against the risks inherent in another.

horizontal spread The simultaneous purchase and sale of an equal number of options of the same class, when the striking prices are the same for each, but expiration dates are different.

in the money In options trading, descriptive of the condition in which current market value of stock is higher than the striking price of a call. The opposite is true of a put option.

income approach An appraisal method used for income property. Value is calculated as a multiplier of rental income earned on similar properties.

insider trading The volume of buy or sell decisions made by corporate officers, major stockholders, and other control persons. This trend is watched by investors and analysts who believe that insiders are in the best position to know about a stock's current and future value.

interest coverage A test of how well a company's earnings allow for the payment of interest. To calculate, divide earnings before interest and taxes, by the total of bond interest.

intermediate trend *See* **Secondary reaction**.

internal rate of return A calculation of yield, computed on the time value of money. The rate assumes that periodic cash receipts—if any—will be reinvested at the same rate of return.

interpolation An estimate of a factor, amount, or rate that falls between two other values. The calculated results from averaging values above and below the desired level.

intrinsic value In options trading, the portion of a contract's premium equal to the dollar value by which the option is in the money.

inverted head-and-shoulders pattern In charting, a bullish trend characterized by three downward movements, with offsetting upward adjustments. The second of three phases (the head) exceeds the first and third (shoulders). *See also* **Head-and-shoulders pattern**.

large block ratio A technical test that follows trends in institutional trades. To calculate, divide the volume in block trading, by total volume.

loan-to-balance ratio (1) In real estate, a comparison of outstanding debt on a property, to appraised value. To calculate, divide the current loan balance by the property's appraised value. (2) The maximum percentage of a property's value for which a lender will grant a mortgage loan. To calculate, divide the loan amount by the purchase price to arrive at the percentage; or multiply a stated percentage by the price, to arrive at the maximum loan.

major trend *See* **Primary movement**.

margin of profit A fundamental test that expresses profits as a percentage of sales. To calculate, divide net operating income by net sales.

market comparison approach An appraisal method in which a property is valued according to recent sales prices for similar properties in the same area.

maturity The date on which a bond will be redeemed.

minor trend In the Dow Theory, the very-short-term price trends, also called *daily fluctuations* or *tertiary trend*.

monthly compounding A method of compounding interest, in which the annual rate is divided by 12, to arrive at a monthly rate.

mortgage constant In real estate, the relationship between debt service and the amount loaned. To calculate, divide annual payments by the original loan amount.

moving average A procedure used in trend analysis, to remove the effects of deviation from the average range of a field. The sum of a field's values are added, and the total is divided by the number of fields in the study. For each new calculation, the oldest period is dropped and the latest period added.

net asset value The net market value of the portfolio of a mutual fund. To calculate, add assets and cash on hand minus liabilities; and divide the result by the number of shares outstanding.

net income ratio A calculation performed for comparisons between mutual funds. Net income is divided by average net assets (average is computed by adding beginning- and ending-year totals of assets, and dividing by 2).

net operating profit Net profit after deducting operating costs and expenses from sales, but before deducting interest and taxes.

new high/new low ratio A technical trend, comparing the number of issues surpassing 52-week trading ranges. To calculate, divide the number of issues reaching new high price levels, by the number with new lows.

nominal yield The stated annual interest rate, based on a bond's par value.

occupancy rate In real estate, the percentage of units being rented out. To calculate, divide the number of occupied units, by total units on the property.

odd-lot balance index A technical indicator used to track odd-lot investor sentiment. To calculate, divide the volume in odd-lot sales, by volume in odd-lot purchases.

odd-lot theory A contrarian technical belief, which holds that the odd-lot investor (one who trades in lots under 100 shares) is usually wrong about market trends. Thus, when odd-lot traders are bullish, the contrarian becomes bearish.

operating ratio *See* **Expense ratio.**

out of the money In options trading, descriptive of the condition in which the current market value of a stock is lower than the striking price of an option.

par value The face value, or redemption value, of a bond or other security.

payout ratio A test of dividends paid as a percentage of adjusted net income. To calculate, divide dividends declared and paid, by adjusted net income (net income less dividends paid to preferred stockholders).

Pi A factor used to compute area, circumference, or volume of circular or cylindrical property; 3.1416.

preferred dividend coverage A test reflecting how well a company's earnings provide for payment of dividends to preferred stockholders. To calculate, divide net income after taxes by preferred dividends.

preferred stock ratio A capitalization test, in which the current value of preferred stock is reflected as a percentage of the total capital. To calculate, divide preferred stock book value, by total capital.

premium bond A bond purchased or with a current market value above par.

present value of 1 The lump sum amount that must be deposited to accumulate a target amount of money in the future, assuming a number of periods, a rate of interest, and a compounding method.

present value of 1 per period An amount that must be on deposit to fund periodic withdrawals for an assumed period of time, based on a rate of interest and compounding method.

pre-tax profit Net profit earned after deducting all costs and expenses from sales, but before deducting the liability for federal income tax.

price/earnings ratio A ratio used to judge relative popularity and demand for stocks. To calculate, divide current market price by the earnings per share.

primary earnings per share The amount a company earns per share of common stock, without allowing for the potential effect of convertible securities.

primary movement In the Dow Theory, a price trend lasting a year or more, establishing an upward (bullish) direction or a downward (bearish) direction; also called a *major trend*.

quarterly compounding A method of compounding interest, in which the annual rate is divided by 4, to arrive at a quarterly rate.

quick-assets ratio A variation of the current ratio, in which inventories are excluded from current assets. To calculate, divide current assets (without inventory) by current liabilities.

radius The distance from the center of a circle to its edge.

Random Walk Hypothesis A theory of market performance stating that all price movement is random and cannot be predicted through either fundamental or technical analysis.

refinancing absorption In real estate, the number of months required to recapture the cost of replacing one loan with another. To calculate, divide the costs of refinancing, by the amount to be saved each month.

relative price-strength ranking An indicator reported by *Investor's Daily* that ranks each stock from 0 to 99, based on volatility trends for the past 12 months.

resistance level In charting, the top price in a stock's current trading range; the assumed highest price that purchasers are willing to pay for shares.

return if cancelled A calculation of option yield, in the event a short option position is closed before expiration date. To calculate, subtract the closing purchase premium from the opening sale premium of the option; add dividends received; and divide the total by the purchase price of stock.

return if exercised A calculation of option yield, in the event the option is exercised. To calculate, subtract the cost of stock from exercise value; add dividends and the amount of option premium received; and divide the total by the purchase price of stock.

return if unchanged A calculation of option yield, in the event the option expires worthless. To calculate, add dividends and option premium received, and divide the sum by the purchase value of stock.

return on invested capital A calculation of yield allowing for earnings of both stockholders and bondholders. To calculate, add net income and interest expense; and divide the sum by shareholders' equity plus the par value of long-term bonds.

rolling techniques In options trading, methods for delaying expiration; increasing or decreasing future striking price; or generating additional premium income. Options may be rolled forward (exchange an option for one with the same striking price, but a later expiration date); rolled down (exchange a contract for one with the same expiration but a lower striking price); rolled up (exchange a contract for one with the same expiration but a higher striking price); or combined (rolled forward and up, or forward and down).

Rule of 72 A rule of thumb for estimating the length of time required to double a deposited sum. To compute, divide 72 by the compound rate of interest.

runaway gap In charting, a substantial price movement that includes gaps between daily trading ranges, often characteristic of panic selling or buying in a security.

secondary reaction In the Dow Theory, a price trend lasting from several weeks to several months, with price movements in a direction opposite that of the primary movement; also called an *intermediate trend*.

semiannual compounding A method of compounding interest, in which the annual rate is divided by 2, to arrive at a semiannual rate.

short-interest theory Also called the *cushion theory*; a belief that changes in short interest positions can be used as buy or sell indicators. As short interest grows, it creates a cushion for future closing purchase transactions.

simple interest Payment of interest on a deposited fund, with no compounding benefits.

simple moving average A method for calculating moving average, in which the oldest period is dropped and the latest added; the total value of all fields is added together, and the sum is divided by the number of fields in the study.

sinking fund payments The amounts that must be deposited over an assumed number of periods, assuming a rate of interest and a compounding method, in order to accumulate a target amount.

spread In options trading, the simultaneous purchase and sale of the same number of options on the same class of the same underlying security; each side has different striking prices, different expiration dates, or both. *See also* **Diagonal spread, Horizontal spread,** *and* **Vertical spread.**

straddle The simultaneous purchase and sale of the same number of call and put option contracts. Striking price and expiration date for all contracts are identical.

striking price In options trading, the price at which the underlying stock must be bought or sold, in the event the option is exercised.

support level In charting, the lowest price in a stock's current trading range; the lowest price that sellers are willing to accept for shares.

tangible net worth A company's net worth after deducting the value of intangible assets.

tax-deferred income Income on which a tax liability will not be due until a future date.

tax-free income Income on which no income tax is due, currently or in the future.

technical analysis A method of selecting investments and timing purchases and sales, based solely on trends established by indexes, investment statistics, and charting patterns.

time value In options trading, the portion of an option contract's premium above any intrinsic value.

time value of money The varying adjusted worth of money, based on compound interest over time. The longer a compound interest period, the greater the time value.

total return (1) In options trading, the yield from a stock and related covered option investment. To calculate, subtract the purchase price of stock from the sales price; add dividends and option premium received; divide the total by the purchase price of stock; and annualize the resultant yield. (2) In real estate, the annualized annual yield from the investment. To calculate, add the total of capital gain (adjusted sales price less adjusted purchase price), and net rental income and tax benefits received; divide that total by the adjusted purchase price; and divide the resulting percentage by the number of years the property was held.

triangle In charting, a price pattern in which volatility widens or narrows; the triangle is used to predict future volatility trends.

vacancy rate In real estate, a method for describing the level of vacant units:
a) Percentage of units vacant: Divide the vacant units by total units on the property.
b) Percentage of dollars lost: Divide the amount of lost income, by total potential income.
c) Percentage of time: Divide the number of months vacant by a full year (12).

vertical spread The simultaneous purchase and sale of an equal number of options, when the striking prices on each side are different, but expiration dates are the same.

volatility A test of price stability in a stock. To calculate, subtract the 52-week low price from the 52-week high; and divide the net by the low.

volume The cubic feet within a three-dimensional shape.

volume of a cylinder The computed cubic feet of a cylindrical property. To calculate, multiply Pi (3.1416), by the square of the radius, and then by the height.

volume of a rectangle The computed cubic feet of a rectangular-shaped property. To calculate, multiply length by width by height.

volume percentage change An indicator reported by *Investor's Daily* showing a 50-day moving average ranking of each security, for volume levels.

weighted appraisal An appraisal combining cost, income, and market comparison approaches, but granting different levels of significance to each method. The total weight assigned to each of the three methods must equal 100%.

weighted moving average A method for computing moving average, in which varying significance is assigned to some fields, over the weight assigned to others. An increasing-weight method grants increasing value to later fields, so that the total weight must be divided by the sum of the field's digits. An alternative is to assign equal weight to all except the latest field, which is given double weight value.

weighted return A calculation of yield on mutual fund investments, when invested sums are held for dissimilar periods. The months in a period are divided by the total holding period; and the result is multiplied by the rate earned. The rates so calculated are then added together to arrive at the weighted return.

working capital Current assets less current liabilities.

working capital turnover The number of times, on average, that working capital is used to produce an annual sales volume. To calculate, divide gross sales by working capital (current assets less current liabilities).

yield on common stock The percentage earned on the basis of dividends paid. To calculate, divide the amount of annual dividends by the current market price of stock.

yield-to-average life A yield calculated on two assumptions: that a current portfolio will not be changed, and that all income earned will be reinvested at the same rate of interest for the average life of the portfolio securities.

yield to maturity A method for calculating yields on bonds purchased at a discount or premium. This is the average yield from two separate calculations: the income earned as a percentage of purchase price, and annual yield as a percentage of par value.

Index